Managing in the New Team Environment

Skills, Tools, and Methods

Managing in the New Team Environment

Skills, Tools, and Methods

Larry Hirschhorn

Wharton Center for Applied Research

 ADDISON-WESLEY PUBLISHING COMPANY, INC.
Reading, Massachusetts • Menlo Park, California • New York
Don Mills, Ontario • Wokingham, England • Amsterdam • Bonn
Sydney • Singapore • Tokyo • Madrid • San Juan

To Marla, my wife, in love,
and to her father and mother, Mac and Doris,
for their unstinting generosity

Library of Congress Cataloging-in-Publication Data

Hirschhorn, Larry.
Managing in the new team environment: skills, tools, and methods/Larry
Hirschhorn.
p.   cm.
ISBN 0-201-52503-8
1. Work groups—Management.   I. Title.
HD66.H57 1991
658.4'036—dc20   90-415
                                                                      CIP

This book is in the Addison-Wesley Series on Organization Development.
Editors: Edgar H. Schein, Richard Beckhard

9 10 11 12 13 14 BAM 00999897

Other Titles in the Organization Development Series

Parallel Learning Structures: Creating Innovations in Bureaucracies
Gervase R. Bushe and A.B. Shani
1991 (52427)

Parallel learning structures are technostructural interventions that promote system-wide change in bureaucracies while retaining the advantages of bureaucratic design. This text serves as a resource of models and theories built around five cases of parallel learning structures that can help those who create and maintain them be more effective and successful. For those new to parallel learning structures, the text provides practical advice as to when and how to use them.

The Strategic Management Process: Integrating the OD Perspective
David Hitchin and Walter Ross
1991 (52429)

Written for CEOs, general managers, OD professionals, and strategic-planning specialists, this text integrates the OD perspective into the strategic-management process. This approach begins with the authors' belief that building and sustaining a healthy, high-performance organization is dependent upon the fact that people are the key to organizational success, and that their management is critical to successful strategic planning and execution. The authors' philosophy and suggestions for the strategic management of both profit and nonprofit organizations are presented.

The Conflict-Positive Organization: Stimulate Diversity and Create Unity
Dean Tjosvold
1991 (51485)

This book describes how managers and employees can use conflict to find common ground, solve problems, and strengthen morale and relationships. By showing how well-managed conflict invigorates and empowers teams and organizations, the text demonstrates how conflict is vital for a company's continuous improvement and increased competitive advantage.

Change by Design
Robert R. Blake, Jane Srygley Mouton, and Anne Adams McCanse
1989 (50748)

This book develops a systematic approach to organization development and provides readers with rich illustrations of coherent planned change. The book involves testing, examining, revising, and strengthening conceptual foundations in order to create sharper corporate focus and increased predictability of successful organization development.

Organization Development in Health Care
R. Wayne Boss
1989 (18364)
This is the first book to discuss the intricacies of the health care industry. The book explains the impact of OD in creating healthy and viable organizations in the health care sector. Through unique and innovative techniques, hospitals are able to reduce nursing turnover, thereby resolving the nursing shortage problem. The text also addresses how OD can improve such bottom-line variables as cash flow and net profits.

Self-Designing Organizations: Learning How to Create High Performance
Susan Albers Mohrman and Thomas G. Cummings
1989 (14603)
This book looks beyond traditional approaches to organizational transition, offering a strategy for developing organizations that enables them to learn not only how to adjust to the dynamic environment in which they exist, but also how to achieve a higher level of performance. This strategy assumes that change is a learning process: the goal is continually refined as organizational members learn how to function more effectively and respond to dynamic conditions in their environment.

Power and Organization Development: Mobilizing Power to Implement Change
Larry E. Greiner and Virginia E. Schein
1988 (12185)
This book forges an important collaborative approach between two opposing and often contradictory approaches to management: OD practitioners who espouse a "more humane" workplace without understanding the political realities of getting things done, and practicing managers who feel comfortable with power but overlook the role of human potential in contributing to positive results.

Designing Organizations for High Performance
David P. Hanna
1988 (12693)
This book is the first to give insight into the actual processes you can use to translate organizational concepts into bottom-line improvements. Hanna's "how-to" approach shows not only the successful methods of intervention, but also the plans behind them and the corresponding results.

Process Consultation, Volume 1: Its Role in Organization Development, Second Edition
Edgar H. Schein
1988 (06736)
How can a situation be influenced in the workplace without the direct use of power or formal authority? This book presents the core theoretical foundations and basic prescriptions for effective management.

Organizational Transitions: Managing Complex Change, Second Edition
Richard Beckhard and Reuben T. Harris

1987 (10887)

This book discusses the choices involved in developing a management system appropriate to the "transition state." It also discusses commitment to change, organizational culture, and increasing and maintaining productivity, creativity, and innovation.

Organization Development: A Normative View
W. Warner Burke

1987 (10697)

This book concisely describes and defines the theories and practices of organization development and also looks at organization development as change in an organization's culture. It is a useful guide to the field of organization development and is invaluable to managers, executives, practitioners, and anyone desiring an excellent overview of this multifaceted field.

Team Building: Issues and Alternatives, Second Edition
William G. Dyer

1987 (18037)

Through the use of the techniques and procedures described in this book, managers and consultants can effectively prepare, apply, and follow up on the human processes affecting the productive functioning of teams.

The Technology Connection: Strategy and Change in the Information Age
Marc S. Gerstein

1987 (12188)

This is a book that guides managers and consultants through crucial decisions about the use of technology for increasing effectiveness and competitive advantage. It provides a useful way to think about the relationship between information technology, business strategy, and the process of change in organizations.

Stream Analysis: A Powerful Way to Diagnose and Manage Organizational Change
Jerry I. Porras

1987 (05693)

Drawing on a conceptual framework that helps the reader to better understand organizations, this book shows how to diagnose failings in organizational functioning and how to plan a comprehensive set of actions needed to change the organization into a more effective system.

Process Consultation, Volume II: Lessons for Managers and Consultants
Edgar H. Schein

1987 (06744)

This book shows the viability of the process consultation model for working with human systems. Like Schein's first volume on process consultation, the second volume focuses on the moment-to-moment behavior of the manager or consultant rather than on the design of the OD program.

Managing Conflict: Interpersonal Dialogue and Third-Party Roles, Second Edition
Richard E. Walton

1987 (08859)

This book shows how to implement a dialogue approach to conflict management. It presents a framework for diagnosing recurring conflicts and suggests several basic options for controlling or resolving them.

Pay and Organization Development
Edward E. Lawler

1981 (03990)

This book examines the important role that reward systems play in organization development efforts. By combining examples and specific recommendations with conceptual material, it organizes the various topics and puts them into a total systems perspective. Specific pay approaches such as gainsharing, skill-based pay, and flexible benefits are discussed and their impact on productivity and the quality of work life is analyzed.

Work Redesign
J. Richard Hackman and Greg R. Oldham

1980 (02779)

This book is a comprehensive, clearly written study of work design as a strategy for personal and organizational change. Linking theory and practical technologies, it develops traditional and alternative approaches to work design that can benefit both individuals and organizations.

Organizational Dynamics: Diagnosis and Intervention
John P. Kotter

1978 (03890)

This book offers managers and OD specialists a powerful method of diagnosing organizational problems and of deciding when, where, and how to use (or not use) the diverse and growing number of organizational improvement tools that are available today. Comprehensive and fully integrated, the book includes many different concepts, research findings, and competing philosophies and provides specific examples of how to use the information to improve organizational functioning.

Career Dynamics: Matching Individual and Organizational Needs
Edgar H. Schein

1978 (06834)

This book studies the complexities of career development from both an individual and an organizational perspective. Changing needs throughout the adult life cycle, interaction of work and family, and integration of individual and organizational goals through human resource planning and development are all thoroughly explored.

Matrix
Stanley M. Davis and Paul Lawrence

1977 (01115)

This book defines and describes the matrix organization, a significant departure from the traditional "one man-one boss" management system. The author notes that the tension between the need for independence (fostering innovation) and order (fostering efficiency) drives organizations to consider a matrix system. Among the issues addressed are reasons for using a matrix, methods for establishing one, the impact of the system on individuals, its hazards, and what types of organizations can use a matrix system.

Feedback and Organization Development: Using Data-Based Methods
David A. Nadler

1977 (05006)

This book addresses the use of data as a tool for organizational change. It attempts to bring together some of what is known from experience and research and to translate that knowledge into useful insights for those who are thinking about using data-based methods in organizations. The broad approach of the text is to treat a whole range of questions and issues considering the various uses of data as an organizational change tool.

Designing Complex Organizations
Jay Galbraith

1973 (02559)

This book attempts to present an analytical framework of the design of organizations, particularly of types of organizations that apply lateral decision processes or matrix forms. These forms have become pervasive in all types of organizations, yet there is little systematic public knowledge about them. This book helps fill this gap.

Organization Development: Strategies and Models
Richard Beckhard

1969 (00448)

This book is written for managers, specialists, and students of management who are concerned with the planning of organization development programs to resolve the dilemmas brought about by a rapidly changing environment. Practiced teams of interdependent people must spend real time improving their methods of working, decision making, and communicating, and a planned, managed change is the first step toward effecting and maintaining these improvements.

Organization Development: Its Nature, Origins, and Prospects
Warren G. Bennis
1969 (00523)
This primer on OD is written with an eye toward the people in organizations who are interested in learning more about this educational strategy as well as for those practitioners and students of OD who may want a basic statement both to learn from and to argue with. The author treats the subject with a minimum of academic jargon and a maximum of concrete examples drawn from his own and others' experience.

Developing Organizations: Diagnosis and Action
Paul R. Lawrence and Jay W. Lorsch
1969 (04204)
This book is a personal statement of the authors' evolving experience, through research and consulting, in the work of developing organizations. The text presents the authors' overview of organization development, then proceeds to examine issues at each of three critical interfaces: the organization-environment interface, the group-group interface, and the individual-organization interface, including brief examples of work on each. The text concludes by pulling the themes together in a set of conclusions about organizational development issues as they present themselves to practicing managers.

About the Author

Larry Hirschhorn is a principal of the Wharton Center for Applied Research in Philadelphia. He consults with business, industry, and government on such issues as organization design, the management process, and design of sociotechnical systems that promote productivity and participation. He has worked with a wide range of organizations, including banks, factories, hospitals, and professional service firms. Currently, he is developing new approaches, tools, and concepts for three increasingly important areas of corporate life: the design of knowledge work, new product development, and creation of cross-functional systems and processes.

Larry Hirschhorn is the author of several books, including *Beyond Mechanization,* a study of automation and work design, *The Workplace Within,* a study of the psychodynamics of organizational life, and *Cutting Back,* an assessment of the dynamics of organizational retrenchment. He is a founding member of the International Society for the Psychoanalytic Study of Organizations and a member of the OD Network, the Family Firm Institute, and the Society for Manufacturing Engineers. He is married to Marla Isaacs and has two children, Aaron and Daniel.

Foreword

The Addison-Wesley Series on Organization Development originated in the late 1960s when a number of us recognized that the rapidly growing field of "OD" was not well understood or well defined. We also recognized that there was no one OD philosophy, and hence one could not at that time write a textbook on the theory and practice of OD, but one could make clear what various practitioners were doing under that label. So the original six books launched what has since become a continuing enterprise, the essence of which was to allow different authors to speak for themselves instead of trying to summarize under one umbrella what was obviously a rapidly growing and highly diverse field.

By the early 1980s the series included nineteen titles. OD was growing by leaps and bounds, and it was expanding into all kinds of organizational areas and technologies of intervention. By this time, many textbooks existed as well that tried to capture the core concepts of the field, but we felt that diversity and innovation were still the more salient aspects of OD.

Now as we move into the 1990s our series includes twenty-seven titles, and we are beginning to see some real convergence in the underlying assumptions of OD. As we observe how different professionals working in different kinds of organizations and occupational communities make their case, we see we are still far from having a single "theory" of organization development. Yet, a set of common assumptions is surfacing. We are beginning to see patterns in what works and what does not work, and we are becoming more articulate about these patterns. We are also seeing the field connecting to broader themes in the organizational sciences, and new theories and theories of practice are being presented in such areas as conflict resolution, group dynamics, and the process of change in relationship to culture. The new titles in the series address current themes directly: Tjosvold's *The Conflict-Positive Organization,* for example, connects to a whole research tradition on the dynamics of collaboration, competition, and conflict; Hirschhorn's *Managing in the New Team Environment* contains important links to psychoanalytic group theory; Bushe and Shani's *Parallel Learning Structures* presents a seminal theory of large-scale organization change based on the institution of parallel systems as change agents; and Hitchin and Ross's *The Strategic Management Process* looks at the connection between strategic planning theory and practice and implementation through OD interventions.

As editors we have not dictated these connections, nor have we asked authors to work on higher-order concepts and theories. It is just happening, and it is a welcome turn of events. Perhaps it is an indication that OD may be reaching a period of consolidation and integration. We hope that we can contribute to this trend with future volumes.

Cambridge, Massachusetts   Richard H. Beckhard
New York, New York   Edgar H. Schein

Preface

Managers throughout industry face the growing challenge of managing in team environments. Much has been written on how employees can take up roles as effective team members, and organizational development practitioners have examined how managers and others can help build a team. But, surprisingly, there is still little written on how the manager's day-to-day behavior should change. How should managers take up their role in team settings, how do they take up their authority as they empower others, how do they help others strike the delicate balance between discipline and freedom, individual and collective achievements, intimacy and distance? Managers will make these choices not in the context of formal team-building sessions or at executive retreats, but in the tug and pull of the daily management process. This book is about that tug and pull and is focused on its many-sided dilemmas. Based on many case studies and examples, the book is designed to help managers understand the social-psychological realities that shape their choices and behaviors. Group life is psychological at its core. People committed to accomplishing tasks must manage the dilemmas of competing with one another, respecting while challenging authority, and supporting teammates while holding them accountable. Team environments intensify these dilemmas, and the new manager must understand them, and be prepared to live with them and inside them.

Acknowledgments

This book grew out of a project sponsored by the central staff of the Management Development Group of IBM. Committed to increasing the level and quality of team work in its sales organizations, factories, and laboratories, IBM educators, led by Sam Lawson and George Johnson, asked the professionals of Ferranti Educational Systems to create an interactive-video program on the challenges and dilemmas of managing in a team environment. Led by Kim Donaldson, Linnea Bailey, and Cathy U. Walls, the Ferranti team asked me to write a text they could use to create a video-based educational program. It was a wonderfully fruitful collaboration. Linnea Bailey, as the quintessential project manager, was both tough and caring, Kim Donaldson was my intellectual critic and companion, and Kathy Walls provided ongoing moral and technical support. Sam Lawson and George Johnson of IBM were demanding clients and in setting high standards for clarity, precision, and fit with IBM's culture, they challenged me to be at my professional best.

I would also like to thank Tom Gilmore, my colleague of fourteen years' standing, who was, as he always is, generous with his time, his thoughts, and his encouragement. His work with teams and organizations continues to stimulate my thinking and practice in important ways. I would also like to thank my other colleagues at the Wharton Center for Applied Research—Vinnie Carroll, Nancy Drozdow, Mal O'Connor, Lynn Oppenheim, Nancy Rourke, and Irene Young—for working to create a team setting and climate that promotes spontaneity and discovery. Finally, Barbara Feinberg, Cathy Brundage, Marie Paro, and Nicole Gerdeman provided invaluable editorial and clerical support.

Philadelphia, Pennsylvania   L.H.

Contents

Introduction

In today's economic environment, you the manager depend more than ever on the team of people you manage. New products, new equipment, new procedures, and new reporting relationships command your attention. You can no longer go it alone, keep control of all the details, have all the good ideas, manage all the key relationships, and use your team to simply execute your orders. If you think you can, you are probably overworked and unproductive.

But if you want to step back, to rely on others, to get out from under the press of one detail after another, how do you know you can trust those you supervise? Can you risk depending on them and hope that they will come through? How do you know they are loyal, knowledgeable, and effective? How can you get them to help each other so that they can ultimately help you? How do you give them needed direction without interfering in their work? How do you lead without directing, and give elbow room without abdicating? How can you appraise and reward their good performance when you have little control over their salary levels? If you expect and get much from them, what do you owe them politically and emotionally? And, finally, as you build your team, how do you ensure that the individuals within it don't get "lost in the crowd"? How can you be each individual's boss while also supporting the team's autonomy?

Team settings challenge your skills as a manager. A factory manager, responsible for the performance of a self-managing team, was worried about its performance. Eager to support its autonomy, he did not know how to confront the team directly. Instead, he told the team "moderator" (a team member who facilitated group meetings) that "whichever team member was qualified in a production skills group where there is a problem should help out ... regardless of their assignment." This puzzled team members, because they were already helping one another out. Was the manager asking team members to specialize in a few jobs rather than rotate assignments as they were allowed to do? A few days later the manager sent a supervisor back to the team, but called him a consultant. One worker responded, "He says he is a consultant, but I know he'll behave like a manager."

What was going on here? The manager was afraid of being direct. Believing that to promote his team's autonomy he had to withhold his thoughts and feelings he was compelled to communicate indirectly. He "softened" the team up, watched their response, and when they failed to improve performance, he sent in a boss, while calling him a consultant. The manager was confused about how to take authority in a team environment, about how to be responsible in his job without undermining the role and authority of team members. Ironically, by being indirect, by trying to protect the workers' "feelings" and self-esteem, he appeared manipulative instead.[1]

Managers used to unilateral authority become confused with the problems of being aggressive, of saying no when they mean it when managing in a team setting. As one worker noted, "Participation means 'guess what is on my mind.'" Another, reflecting on the process of giving input to managers, said, "An answer of 'no' to a suggestion always begins with the phrase, 'But are you sure you have considered these additional factors.'"[2] Moreover, in managing this dilemma some managers simply abdicate. One plant manager of a large, 3,000-member electronics plant faced very complicated strategic and operational issues. He introduced a just-in-time system; he eliminated the punch clock and the time-and-motion group; he worked to integrate customer services, production control, and operations. Facing significant stress, the plant community needed his leadership. Yet, in addressing a large group of managers and supervisors, he noted that while he once thought he was their coach he now considered himself to be their cheerleader. The metaphor was compelling. Just when he was pushing the factory to transform itself, to be more self-managing while also developing new relationships

---

1. J. Maxwell Eden, "Democracy at Work for a More Participatory Politics," University of California, Los Angeles, 1979, pp. 239–240.

2. John Witte, *Democracy, Authority, and Alienation at Work* (Chicago: University of Chicago Press, 1980), p. 119.

among its divisions and departments, he was going to step to the side.

Indeed, caught by the challenge of saying both "yes" and "no" in new ways, of affirming both the teams' and their own authority, many managers oscillate between the dictatorial "no" and the abdicating "yes." Describing a plant manager in charge of a self-managing team system, one coordinator noted, "He oscillated between being participative and being a little Caesar. He did not know how to lead in a plant based on the team concept."

This book is designed to help manage these tensions and cope with these complexities. Based on an interactive video course developed at IBM, it takes you step-by-step through the process of building your team and authorizing team members to act, while you learn to step back and delegate.

If you are like many managers schooled in the old ways and socialized in conventional company settings, you've probably internalized one command without question: *"Stay in control."* This powerful command and its associated dictums ("When you don't know, don't ask," "Don't look weak") may have worked in the days when you could master all the details of your unchanging job, when subordinates expected and wanted their managers to know it all, when people never questioned authority, and when paternalistic companies protected their employees in exchange for their unquestioning loyalty.

But the world of work has changed. You need to leave this "control orientation" behind and take what this book describes as the "learner role." In taking the learner role, you will become not only a more effective manager but also a more effective subordinate and colleague. As you learn to be a learner, your capacity to acquire knowledge and enroll others in your work and interests will grow dramatically. But as the book also shows, taking the learner role creates risks and entails work. The book will help you prepare for these risks and do this work so that as you promote your team's development you are fostering your own as well.

In the past, you could rely on common sense, your instincts, and your familiarity with your team members to manage in a team environment. But just as companies need more sophisticated financial-tracking mechanisms to control money flows as they grow, you too need new techniques to keep the team process on track and ensure that empowered individuals are harnessed to the team effort. The rest of this book is geared to teach you the techniques for managing in a team environment. They range from tools designed to help groups solve problems to methods of observation and tips on intervention when you are facilitating a team discussion. But if you try to apply these techniques from the control role in the hope of producing "perfect performances" and a flawless presentation of yourself, you will be disappointed. In dealing with the intensely interpersonal world of teams, no technique is foolproof, and no technique can control the contingencies of an all-too-human world. Abraham Zaleznik, the management theorist, tells the story of a CEO who found that her subordinates were meticulous in preparing budgets and compliant in following the rules, but were unconnected emotionally to the whole process. The driving rhythms of the budget cycle and the abstract language of numbers and tables made it difficult for the team to talk about the core issues of technology and markets that preoccupied managers day to day. Understanding this situation, the CEO noted, "I need the numbers, but more importantly, I need executives with a fire in their bellies to accomplish something in their business that will make them and their people proud."[3]

In other words, techniques severed from their human context are lifeless and ineffective. The more you hope to control others and yourself through techniques, and the more you act upon such hopes, the less collaborative and more manipulative you will seem to those around you. Like the craftsman's tools, techniques amplify your effort, your judgments, your instincts, and your empathetic responses—but they can't substitute for them.

The book is divided into five chapters and a summary. The first chapter introduces you to the nature of the new team. With this understanding in hand, Chapter 2 invites you to learn how to give your team the *structure*—the boundaries—it needs to do its work, and Chapter 3 shows you how to facilitate the team's basic *processes*. By mastering the techniques and tools you need to provide your team with both a viable structure and process, you will be able to create an empowered team that supports your work.

The fourth chapter then refocuses your attention on the needs of each individual team member. Emphasizing that each team member has a relationship to you as well as to the team, the chapter shows

---

3. Abraham Zaleznik, *The Management Mystique* (New York: Harper & Row, 1989), p. 95.

how you can supervise and support individual team members and how you can acknowledge the differences among them while also supporting and strengthening their interrelationships.

The fifth chapter brings the argument of the book together by showing how its themes and arguments are linked to the concept of the "learner role." Acknowledging that managing in a team environment puts you in the middle of a series of paradoxes, the chapter shows how you can master these paradoxes by taking up the learner rather than the control role. By learning to explore your setting and collaborating with just those people who at first appear to be the "cause" of your problems, you acknowledge your role in these problems and get others to help you solve them.

Finally, the last chapter summarizes the argument of the book and describes the characteristics of the team you will help create and sustain if you follow the book's guidelines.

The following diagram highlights the book's logical flow of argument.

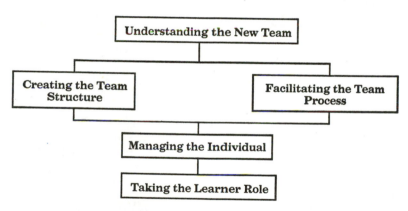

A political philosopher once said, "The perfect is the enemy of the good." This sounds paradoxical. Aren't we always searching for the better, more perfect accomplishment? Of course we are. But in doing so we are bound to stumble, to uncover our own limitations and flaws. If we regard these flaws as shameful, we will deny ourselves the experiences and experiments we need to obtain a more perfect accomplishment. Applying the lessons of this book to your own experience, you, like all learners, will make mistakes. But in working through these mistakes you will not only become a more sophisticated manager in the team environment, you will invite your team members to take risks without fear of shaming themselves as well. This style of leadership is one hallmark of a culture that supports innovation.

1

Understanding the New Team

Key Concepts: Balancing empowerment and collaboration in the team process; thoughts and feelings in the life of the team; managing the triangle comprised by the individual, the manager, and the team.

Balance Empowerment with Collaboration

The governor had assembled an unusually talented advisory group, composed of a finance director, a lawyer and expert on urban poverty, and a skilled liaison to the state legislature. Yet despite the talent each member possessed, the group never jelled as a working collective, and outsiders were struck by the way in which the "whole was less than the sum of its parts." Unable to collaborate, each person assumed that he or she knew best what the governor was "really" thinking, which, not surprisingly, matched their own personal perspectives. Moreover, while each member of the team imagined that he or she was more committed to the governor than the others were, the finance director was most distrusted. "She is a carpetbagger," some would say, "simply here in the state to build her resume." But the finance director believed that, in the face of the state's fiscal crisis, she was simply performing the black-hat role, which no one else wanted to either honor or authorize. My sense is that the finance director was a scapegoat for everyone's feelings, that the group was not really a collective."

Consultant to the governor

If you are schooled in the old ways, you learned how to be a team player, but it was team of a particular sort. In his 1950s study of large corporations, William Whyte coined the phrase "Organization Man."[1] He suggested that managers anxious to protect their careers had learned to conform to top management's way of thinking and acting. Awed by the power and success of the managerial elites who led the American economy through its decades of world dominance, few managers wanted to rock the boat. Instead, they had their radar out to see what top executives wanted, and they complied. *They wanted to be team players, to conform.*

As many analysts have suggested, this kind of team—this culture of conformity—inhibited people's ability to think critically and creatively and contributed significantly to the declining competitiveness of American industry. The auto industry—and particularly the General Motors Corporation—exemplifies this process.[2] Many analysts who have examined the current dilemmas of the U.S. automobile industry have been struck by its unresponsiveness to signs of change and competition. Beginning with the "invasion" of the Volkswagen Bug in the early sixties, followed by the gasoline shortages in the seventies and the consumer's demand for quality goods in the eighties, the automobile industry has had three decades in which to retool, realign its relationships to customers, and develop better relationships with its work force. Yet it seems that the industry has been largely reactive to competition and slow to restructure its relationships to key stakeholders.

The culture of teams based on conformity played a significant role here. For example, the executive-level social system at General Motors was a closed one. People who wanted to be promoted had to be male, live in fashionable suburbs of Detroit, join the right golf

---

1. William H. Whyte, *The Organization Man* (New York: Simon & Schuster, 1956).

2. For a general understanding of the emotional climate that shapes such conformity, see Howard Schwartz, "On the Psychodynamics of Organizational Totalitarianism," *Journal of Management* 4(2) (1987): 24–28.

clubs, and commit their wives to social activity within the company. General Motors was their world. The upwardly mobile manager who joined the culture felt privileged and powerful to be on the inside. But in exchange for this privilege, he shut down his ability to think critically. Lacking the challenge of criticism within the upper levels of the company, senior executives helped create a system that promoted feelings of specialness and arrogance. This was why Charles Wilson, the president of GM during the Eisenhower years, could say ingenuously, "What is good for General Motors is good for the country," as if the conflicts and problems that General Motors had created—the planned obsolescence of its cars, the counter-productive labor-relations systems it sponsored—were not as important as its contributions. Thus, when faced with its first real competition in almost fifty years, this arrogance, generated by the company's insularity and system of conformity, often led General Motors' managers to blame others for the company's competitive problems. If General Motors was losing market share, it was because labor was irresponsible, the Japanese were competing unfairly, or the customer expected too much. Conformity and arrogance inhibited creative thinking.

Today you want a different kind of team. As you supervise larger numbers of people, and as rapid changes in product lines and technologies require you to rely on the initiatives of team members, you need to *authorize* individuals in the team to think for themselves, come up with new ideas, try alternative approaches—in other words, be nonconformists. But here is the rub: You need to get these independent thinkers to work together, to coordinate their efforts. *Yet the more people in the group think for themselves, the more complicated is the task of getting them to work together.* As the brief vignette on the governor's cabinet suggests, a group of talented people each feeling authorized in their own professions and roles can actually create an ineffective team. Moreover, because each person assumed that he or she could best represent the governor, the governor's own authority was undermined. The different perspectives he needed to perform his role with authority—legal, social, financial, and political—were never brought together by the group. Their fragmentation led to his weakness.

Using or Suppressing Thoughts and Feelings

I really learned to be a supervisor when I got one team to think that they were a work team, not a family group. I made a list for them of what groups were. I told them they don't have to like each other. I introduced task-focused skills that would help them get the job done.

Supervisor in a factory

Abraham Zaleznik tells the story of a manager who, because he was angry at his staff for failing to meet a schedule, did not tell them he was angry but simply held them back one Friday afternoon, ruining dinner and weekend plans. The staff "got the message," but it was communicated with such bitterness that it further disconnected the manager from his employees. The manager's fear of expressing anger only created a more chronically angry situation.[3]

In the old world of teams, of conforming members, people solved the problem of working in groups by clamming up, by suppressing their thoughts and feelings, by going along to get along. This worked because the stakes in cooperating were not great. As long as people did all their jobs and did not get in each other's way, top-management controls, systems, and policies integrated their efforts. But in today's team environment people have to get in each others' way to get their work done; they can no longer rely on you and on corporate policies to integrate their work.

Think of the product-development process. If top management wants to accelerate the rate of product development, design engineers, marketing people, and manufacturing managers have to work closely together testing and challenging each other's assumptions. If the marketing person thinks the engineer is overdesigning the product, she cannot withhold criticism in the interests of peace. If the engineer feels that the marketing person is being too abstract, is talking about "trends and markets" rather than about uses and consumers, then he cannot suppress his doubts because he does not want to make waves. If people don't step forward and say what they are thinking and feeling—"I am worried," "This is confusing me," "You are being unclear," "I feel like you are ignoring me"—early mistakes or missed opportunities in the design process will never be corrected.

---

3. Abraham Zaleznik, *The Management Mystique* (New York: Harper & Row, 1989), p. 118.

Similarly, consider the following common experience. Unsure of the competence of his design team, a top executive holds an early design review for a promising new product. Wary of communicating his real feelings, because he does not want the team to lose confidence, he justifies the early review by saying that he just "wants to help." The design-team manager, surprised by the early review, fears that the executive is losing confidence in her. She decides therefore to put on a really "good show" and to suppress any doubts she has about the product or any problems she is facing in the design process.

The meeting takes place, and everyone walks around their thoughts and feelings. The senior executive asks pointed, tough questions without ever saying, "I am worried, do you really know what you are doing?" The design-team manager parries with snappy answers that obscure some of the problematic issues she faces. *As a result, no one learns anything from the meeting.* The key design issues are not discussed, the executive and manager mistrust one another even more, and the design process is potentially undermined.

Thus, to work and manage effectively in the new team environment, people must learn to use their inner thoughts and feelings in the service of getting work done. As the quote by the factory supervisor suggests, the point of a team is not to make everyone feel happy or close, nor are feelings important simply because they help team members feel intimate. Rather, the thoughts and feelings people typically suppress are important guides and aids in helping the team accomplish its work. If the engineer's anxiety that the marketing person is being too abstract is communicated, it can help clarify where the two typically "turn each other off" with abtract language or specialized terms. If the executive and design manager are more direct with each other, they can tackle the design challenges they both face, but are reluctant to discuss.

Missteps in the Dance

I forward questions from my shop people to engineers at a weekly meeting of my line. One question phrased in general terms, but in fact describing the behavior of one specific engineer, asked, "If the specifications are important, why do you sign off without investigation?" The engineer, who had in fact signed off some lots even though they were out of spec, got defensive, refused to sign off on anything even with an investigation, and ended up not speaking to me or coming into the shop for weeks. Only after two months is our prior relationship being restored. The point is the shop needs its questions answered. If I had run roughshod over him I could understand his attitude, but the question was not asked in an aggressive manner. My shop can't stop functioning to protect someone's ego.

Factory supervisor

Using our thoughts and feelings to get work done challenges our courage and sensitivity. Our feelings can confuse us, and sometimes when we hope to be direct we can unintentionally be circuitous. In linking authority with collaboration we are playing with fire. In the vignette, the supervisor hopes to challenge the engineer who signs off on specifications carelessly. Yet he does it indirectly, and without personal authority. He forwards the operators' questions rather than speaking for himself, and he asks the question in general terms, though it is clear it is directed to only one engineer. The engineer, ashamed to be so exposed in front of everybody without being directly acknowledged, reacts petulantly by slowing up the operators' work. The supervisor complains that the shop can't stop to protect someone's ego, but it seems that the supervisor has gone to great length to protect his own ego. Afraid to confront the engineer himself, he used the group meeting, and an anonymous question, as a defense against the aggressive feelings he would have had to mobilize to talk to the engineer one-on-one. Like the engineer, he too disliked feeling exposed and perhaps shamed. Thus while complaining about the engineer's sensitive ego, he may have been in fact protecting his own. It is not uncommon for people who are afraid or anxious to attribute what they are feeling to someone else.

This case highlights the fact that direct talk is far from simple. People worry about challenging each other, they fear being aggressive, and they are concerned about losing control over their own reactions. Reacting defensively and attributing their feelings or dilemmas to others, they hurt each other. Thus to balance authority and collaboration, you and your team must master the protocols of direct talk. Developing the necessary skills requires practice and an overall orientation toward your role that allows you to experiment. This book will show you how. But even having mastered these ideas and skills you will not become the perfect team leader. Missteps in the dance, and your recovery from them, are often the only way to figure out what is going on. So as you begin to learn how to manage in a team environment, don't try to create the "perfect" team with no conflicts, differences, politics, or disappointments. Rather, try to create a mature team that acknowledges what is difficult about sophisticated team dynamics and that harnesses people's thoughts and feelings to the team's work.

The following table should give you a feeling for the dimensions of your new task as manager in the new team environment.

Old Environment	New Environment
Person followed orders.	Person comes up with initiatives.
Group depended on manager.	Group has considerable authority to chart its own steps.
Group was a team because people conformed to direction set by manager. No one rocked the boat.	Group is a team because people learn to collaborate in the face of their emerging right to think for themselves. People rock the boat *and* work together.
People cooperated by suppressing their thoughts and feelings. They wanted to get along.	People cooperate by using their thoughts and feelings. They link up through direct talk.

The Triangle

When talking to people here about our new team system I don't use the word "empower" at all. The last plant manager here used to walk around saying, "You can control your destiny." Now that was pie in the sky. The most an operator can do is walk out and quit. I say to people, ask me questions and don't be afraid to challenge me, in my office or at staff meetings.

Plant manager of an electronics plant

To manage in the team environment you need to learn how to involve and engage your group of subordinates in the important decisions you need to make. If successful, your subordinates will view you as a "member of the team" as much as a manager of it. But however open and participative you are, and however successful you are in becoming a member of the team, the fact that you are the manager of the group, that you appraise the performance of each of its members, will always differentiate you from group members. The manager described in the Introduction entertained the fantasy that by empowering his team in the plant he could become its cheerleader and so step to the sideline. Not only does he deny that he is different from them, but he joins the team passively. By contrast, the plant manager just quoted has recoiled from the language of empowerment. She acknowledges the difference between her and her subordinates but says that to live inside the team system people must be able to challenge one another across the authority boundary.

All of your subordinates take your official role very seriously, even if you want to "join the team." The fact that you are at least one level higher in the organizational hierarchy than the members of your team means that each of your team members will have a distinctive and unique relationship to you when contrasted to the relationships they have with one another. If you try to manage in the team environment by pretending that the differences in status and power between you and your team members do not matter, you are bound to be disappointed. Your challenge is to create an open and participative process in the face of, and by acknowledging, this difference.

It is useful to think of your role as manager in a team environment by thinking of yourself as taking a role in a triangle of relationships. Look at the following diagram.

At any given moment, there are at least three different kinds of relationships operating in your setting: your relationship to each of the team members as individuals, your relationship to the team as a whole, and each individual's relationship to the team as a whole. Often the problems of managing in a team environment emerge when managers fail to recognize how these relationships can affect one another. Think of the following:

1. Two members of the team want to compete for your attention at a team meeting, so when discussing options for a particular decision, they dominate the team discussion, crowding out other team members.

2. A team member, feeling that you have been unfair in a recent appraisal session, makes unhelpful and skeptical comments in a group discussion. You feel as if he is leading a fight against you in the group.

3. The team seems passive and uninvolved, even though you are trying to involve them in a decision. It turns out that the team members are unhappy that you have not been harder on one member who has failed to contribute to the team's efforts.

In each of these three cases, relationships along one leg of the triangle are affected by relationships along another. Your role as the manager of each individual team member cannot be separated from your role as the manager of the team. Similarly, team members' relationships to one another cannot be separated from their relationship to you.

Looking at the triangle it is useful to think of how it may become unbalanced. For example:

You pay too much attention to your role as manager of the whole team.

You neglect some members' feelings that you are not acknowledging their distinctive contributions.

Some members withhold their best thinking from the team.

The team seems passive and uninvolved.

You feel that the team is "ungrateful" because here you have been emphasizing how you want to be the manager to the *whole* team, and they are not responding.

Similarly,

> You pay too much attention to your individual relationships to each of the team members.
>
> Many team members feel that they have a special relationship to you.
>
> Some team members feel that they can represent your authority in the group, that they are the team's rightful leaders.
>
> It is difficult for team members to work together.
>
> You, therefore, justify your neglect of the team as a whole, since after all they can't work together.

As these examples suggest, you can create traps for yourself by focusing on only one leg of the triangle. To avoid such traps you need binocular vision, you need to look at both your relationship to the group as a whole and your relationship to each individual team member.

In Sum

To manage in a team environment you must balance empowerment with collaboration. This means abandoning the old concept based on conformity, and creating a setting where people, authorized to think for themselves, are also able to collaborate with one another. This means that by using rather than suppressing thoughts and feelings, you and team members must learn the art of direct talk. Such talk will not create a "family" nor make everyone feel intimate, but it will help people accomplish their work. However, as the team manager you are in the end not a member of the team. Your role, your higher authority, means that all team members are involved in two interwoven relationships: one to the team as a whole, and one to you as the boss.

2

Creating Team Structure

Key Concepts: Defining the team's environment; shaping an operating philosophy; measuring and rewarding performance; promoting an effective system of roles.

Defining the Environment: Managing the Boundary

President: "It has been a hard year here. Usually, I'm calm, I know there are ups and downs in our business, but for the first time I felt worried and afraid."

Vice President: "Why did you keep these thoughts to yourself—we can all help in thinking this through."

President: "I keep on thinking that it's my role to do all the worrying—the rest of you have to work."

> *Conversation observed at staff meeting of a start-up computer services company*

My rating went from satisfactory to unsatisfactory, even though my performance had been the best yet, people had written letters of commendation, and I had met all my goals. In a conversation with my boss I said that I had been rated down because I was already too far into the pay scale, some of my peers had not had a raise, and our department could award only so many satisfactory ratings. My boss agreed, and said I could take it up with his boss. His boss had already agreed, but then did nothing! I wanted to be rated where I should have been even if I couldn't get a raise.

> *Manager in a telephone office*

17

The first conversation highlights some of the dilemmas that managers and their subordinates face as they confront the wider environment for the unit, the division, or the business as whole. The president of the start-up believes that he has to do most of the worrying and that he must contain most of his anxiety about the state of the business so that others are free to apply their skills to solving problems. The vice president, while not disagreeing with this presumption, wonders if the president has not been too alone in his work. There is no clear answer here, of course, but the conversation highlights how a manager must wrestle with the challenge of managing the boundary of the team, of creating a structure and context for the team so that team members can focus on the challenges they face to improve operations and test new ideas.

Managing in the team environment, you want to give your employees plenty of elbow room to take charge. But in delegating authority to them, you don't abdicate to them. They can't do their work unless they understand the basic objectives of the team, have the resources to do the work, and know how they are performing as a team. As the manager, you are the team's gatekeeper, assuring that the team is effectively linked to the broader corporate environment that shapes its work. You stand at a boundary communicating the company's needs to the team and the team's needs to the company. Team members can manage the work, but you manage the boundary. Indeed, one advantage for you in taking your role as manager in the team environment is that you can become more effective at just such boundary-management tasks, while your employees become more effective at accomplishing basic team objectives.

To manage the boundary effectively, you have to perform three core tasks effectively: ensure that the team understands your operating philosophy; effectively give the team feedback on its performance; and negotiate for the resources the team needs to do its work.

What is complicated about boundary management? Basically you face the dilemmas of "middleness." On the one hand, you are a good corporate citizen; you want the team to be linked to its corporate context and to help it meet broader corporate objectives. On the other hand, you need to protect and defend the team; you have to support them, and you have to show them that you want to get them the resources and information they need. If they feel that you overpromise to your boss and therefore commit them to excessive work that they can accomplish only at great cost to themselves, they will feel that you are unfairly exploiting them. You may force extra work out of them in the short-term, but their commitment to you and willingness to support you will decrease over the longer run. But, if you go to bat for them and sometimes limit their commitments, they will make an extra effort to work "smarter" and more efficiently. Over the longer run, their capacity for work will grow.

Fred, the vice president and plant manager of a large electronics plant, lost credibility because he could not manage effectively from the middle. His plant shipped many of its chips to a key internal customer, another company plant, which used the chips to build circuit boards. Henry, the manager of the second plant, was constantly calling Fred, the manager of the first plant, to complain about shipping delays, even though the pattern of his orders was designed to give his own plant substantial slack when facing customer demands further upstream. Unable to make his own process more efficient, Henry demanded that Fred's plant produce to inventory so that Henry, given his own inefficiencies and wastage, would never be caught short. Fred complied, putting a great deal of pressure on his department heads and production supervisors. Sensing that Fred could not protect them from such an irrational order process—could not, for example, appeal to his and Henry's common superior—Fred's subordinates began to doubt his capabilities. Fred had failed to manage the boundary.

Similarly, recall the situation portrayed in the second chapter-opening vignette. In that scenario, the office manager ceased to believe in the fairness and integrity of his boss and his boss's boss. The first boss simply abdicated, as if to suggest "I only work here," and the second did nothing, either. The manager believes that she has been unfairly treated, but more importantly, she believes that her supervisors do not want to risk their own careers or comfort to ensure that their subordinates are treated fairly. They simply passed her up the chain of command.

These dilemmas of being in the middle (with pressure from above and below) highlight the complicated challenge of managing the boundary, of being the team's gatekeeper. To see how you can meet this challenge, let's see how you can perform the three components of boundary management: establishing a strategy and operating philosophy, giving the team information on its performance, and negotiating for resources. To perform these three components, you and your team will ultimately have to address six questions.

1. Who is in our stakeholder environment and what do they want?
2. What are our objectives in trying to satisfy our stakeholders?
3. What principles of action, what strategy, will we use to achieve these objectives?
4. In implementing this strategy, what ongoing contradictions and trade-offs do we confront?
5. What guidelines should we use to manage these trade-offs, and why have we chosen them?
6. What roles do each of us have in implementing these guidelines, what is the distinctive role of the manager when compared to the role of team members?

Let us examine the three components of boundary management and see how they are based on answers to these questions.

Strategy and Operating Philosophy

Team members often know their jobs very well, but lack a sense of how their jobs affect one another and how these jobs fit into a larger team effort. As a manager, you are often the integrator, ensuring, for example, that the efforts of the engineer, the set-up machinist, and the maintenance worker are consistent with one another. You have much to gain if the team members themselves can spontaneously perform this work of integration. You will be less in the middle and will provide team members with a chance to take on broader roles rather than just perform their narrow jobs.

To help team members coordinate their efforts you must help them understand your operating philosophy, your strategy for the team. Such a philosophy or strategy clarifies what you think is important, what trade-offs you are willing to make, and which stakeholders you regard as important and why. As a manager in the middle you have only a limited effect on the company's mission, but you do have much to say about how your team fits into and supports that mission.

The Limits of Mission Statements

What are the elements of a strategy or an operating philosophy for your team? It is easy to be confused about the meaning of the terms "mission" and "strategy." Managers writing mission statements often wind up producing "apple pie-and-motherhood" sentences ("Our mission is to do quality work, to satisfy our internal customers, to support corporate objectives"), none of which clarifies how actual operating activity and decisions are to be shaped by the mission. The problem with such mission statements is that they cannot be logically negated. Who would say that our mission is "not to do quality work," "not to satisfy our internal customers," or "not to support corporate objectives"? Work units do have a mission—ultimately they do have to meet objectives, such as production levels, quality of service, and productivity growth—but they need an operating philosophy, a strategy, to accomplish these objectives. In the absence of a strategy, the mission is an empty statement, a platitude that covers up a series of conflicts rather than clarifying a series of choices.

Nike: Three Principles

Consider by way of example the Nike shoe company.[1] Nike experienced enormous growth over a short period of time, starting up with a minimum amount of capital in 1964 and generating sales of $700 million by 1982. This growth was built upon a clear and simple strategy developed and formulated when the company was founded. Two elements were key. First, the company would rely on contractors in the Far East for actual production of the athletic shoes. By staying out of production, Nike executives could focus on their customers. Second, Nike executives, steeped in the world of sports, would develop long-term relationships with famous athletes, based on the principles of mutuality and reciprocity. While Nike wanted the athletes to wear its shoes and promote their use, the company would not simply treat them as "cash cows" to be disposed of when they lost their usefulness. Nike executives believed that such relationships were consistent with their own personal commitments to athletes and athletics, and that that commitment would in the long run lead athletes to feel committed to Nike.

---

1.   See Harvard Business School Case 385–025, 1984.

The Nike example highlights some key features of an operating philosophy. First, the Nike executives had a good working knowledge of the "stakeholder" environment in which they had to compete. As a result of their experience in the early years of building the business, they understood the motives and capabilities of their contractors in the Far East, the distribution channels for sneakers, and the emerging popular culture of athletic activity. Second, understanding their stakeholder environment, they developed a strategy that, like a magnetic field, gave them direction and orientation within it. They knew where to place themselves in it—away from production and close to the final customer—and what kinds of relationships they wanted with each of the key stakeholders (long-term ones with distributors, less committed ones with contractors). Third, this orientation helped them shape a set of working guidelines or principles, such as, "If you have to lose money to protect our links to the athletes we've worked with, then do so," or, "Find ways to reduce the risks our distributors face; we need to conserve our marketing channels to our customers."

Thus, an operating philosophy, or strategy, is more than a statement of platitudes, but rather is based on the team's understanding of its stakeholder environment. It orients people within that team, helping them see what is key and what needs to be emphasized. It links the unit's mission to ongoing operations. Like a magnetic field, it orients the different team members, who after all have different roles and perspectives, so that they are pushing in the same direction. If they know why they are working, what stakeholders they have to satisfy, which efforts have priority, and which aspects of their work are most important, they can manage their own work, and thus work with one another more effectively.

Strategy, Objectives, and Guidelines

Strategy helps make objectives come alive. Managers frequently create objectives for their teams—"We will sell so much product," We will train so many people"—but in the absence of a strategy for accomplishing these objectives, the objectives themselves remain abstract and lifeless.

Consider the following example. The manager of a maintenance group wants his team to limit downtime to 5 percent of operating time. To make this objective real, to situate this objective in the team's ongoing relationships with the plant, the manager needs a strategy for minimizing downtime. The strategy, or operating philosophy, might be based on the following principles.

1. When making a maintenance call, try to teach the user something about the machine—even if this lengthens the time of the call.

2. Assess historical data on machine performance; identify the set of machines that account for 80 percent of the calls and develop a specific preventive-maintenance program for them. Get to the machine before the user has to call you.

3. Identify one person in each department who has a particular interest in the "insides" of its machines. Involve that person in maintenance-planning meetings.

These are principles of *action,* not descriptions of goals. They say that maintenance people should *educate* users, *target* difficult areas, and *collaborate* with users in planning. A strategy complements a mission by specifying the modes of action for linking the team to its stakeholders.

Guidelines and Trade-offs

Consider the problem that many computer sales teams face. A customer wants a particular computer and software system to handle inventory. Examining the situation, the salesperson feels that the customer will quickly outgrow this system and should wait until a more developed version of the computer system is available. Should the salesperson sell the customer what the customer wants or what he or she feels the customer needs?

This dilemma of "needs versus wants" is common in many sales settings, and depends ultimately on the company's concept of the business environment. If they believe they are in the "relationship" business, where customers want to buy long-term assistance and consultation as well as particular product, and the customers are willing to pay for this extra service, then it makes sense for the salesperson to "educate" the customer and take the risk of losing a present sale in order to build the relationship. If, by contrast, the company and salesforce compete in a "commodity" business where products are not branded and differ only in price, it may be sensible to sell the customer what he or she wants. Since customers don't want to pay a price differential reflecting differences in the way a sale is serviced, the salesforce and the company may lose sales and money if they try to "educate" the customer and develop a long-term relationship. Clearly, individual salespeople do not know how to manage the trade-off between "needs versus wants" or "sales now versus sales later" unless their team and their manager understand the business similarly and have developed a shared set of guidelines.

Similarly, consider the following. A self-managing team of technicians in a pilot plant had to create and implement a schedule of experimental production runs to see if and how new chemicals could be produced economically. Typically, different engineers in the R&D organization asked for "run time" to test their chemicals and the team had to plan a six-week schedule of runs to accommodate these different requests. Taking each engineer's estimate of how much run time was required, they created a schedule that fit each engineer's needs.

Unfortunately, the engineers could not estimate run times effectively, and this disrupted the technicians' schedule. Planning to complete a run in one week, the technicians found instead that they needed two, but nonetheless had to stop to accommodate the next run. Thus they were constantly stopping in the middle of runs, starting new ones, and then returning to old ones when they had time. This made it very difficult for them to learn about the properties of any particular run, because by starting and stopping they lost information, repeated steps, and frequently formed an entirely new subteam of technicians to start up an old run. Thus they decided to implement a new principle of action, a new strategy: "Don't stop a run until it is completed, even if this means delaying another engineer's run." Based on a strategy for meeting the engineers' requests—*complete runs*—this guideline helped the technicians adjust their schedule when facing the inevitable delays in starting new runs.

Guidelines and Roles

Due to a sequence of events over a several-month period of time, a product was backscheduled and on the "critical product" report. The supervisor and I were working on a plan to get the product off the critical list and resume normal delivery schedules.

During the course of our discussions I was arguing for accepting more requests for delivery during the next few weeks. The supervisor did not believe we could accept any more than what was already promised. When the capacity of the various pieces of equipment was analyzed, it appeared that there was sufficient capacity. The number of people appeared to be adequate, although somewhat tight. I therefore asked the supervisor for specifics of where he thought the problem might be. He could give me no specific answer. I concluded that we could accept more program. He agreed, but I felt that he didn't really believe it could be done.

I found this experience to be frustrating, because I felt there was something the supervisor wasn't telling me. He definitely didn't appear to believe we could make the program. He was only agreeing because I was "browbeating" him into doing so.

Department manager in a factory

In every stakeholder field there are contradictions and trade-offs. Team strategy is a maxim, a set of guidelines for acting in the face of these contradictions. For example, plant managers face the recurring and common problem of balancing quality and schedule. Other divisions or internal customers want the product "right now," but the plant manager, supervisors, and workers know that to send it off right now is to risk sending off poor-quality products and materials. How should the plant manager orient herself and her subordinates in a given stakeholder field? Much depends on the plant's conception of the field. If quality is key, and faulty products cannot be easily returned and replaced, then the plant manager will decide to "tilt" toward quality.

But then what happens when internal customers complain about delays? The plant manager as the manager of the boundary must take up the responsibility of managing the consequences of delays. She may, for example, simply take the heat from the complaining internal customer; she may suggest that she and the customer meet with their common boss to assess why requests for orders are creating so much production pressure; she may develop systems that help her unit get advance warning of production requests; or she may invest in a set of technologies or methods, such as just-in-time, or in-line inspection, to help reduce the conflict between schedules and quality. This means that when working with your team to develop guidelines for acting within a stakeholder field, you are also dividing up the work of implementing these guidelines. Your subordinates follow the guidelines, while you stay at the boundary to manage the consequences of their actions and decisions.

Confusion about guidelines, a unit's overall strategy, and the roles that a manager and team members take in implementing them can erode the ties between the manager and his or her subordinate. Consider the case that opened this section. The department manager wants the supervisor to accept more request for production; the supervisor, while agreeing, seems to do so grudgingly, as if he were being browbeaten. When a person withholds thoughts and feelings from another as the supervisor seems to have done, it is a sign of mistrust. The supervisor does not say what he is really thinking or feeling because he cannot trust the manager's intentions. While we don't have access to supervisor's feelings, it is likely that he is thinking such thoughts as, "Is the manager asking for more production simply because he wants to look good to his bosses? Will he sandbag me if I can't deliver? What if I really stick to my guns and say no—will he find ways to punish me? If he knows the answer he wants to hear, why is he is asking? Why not just tell me?"

In managing the common pressures of quality, resources, and deliveries that all production units experience, the manager and his supervisor have not developed a shared sense of the stakeholder environments they face, their respective roles within it, and the guidelines they will both implement to reinforce each other's decisions and actions.

Starting the Conversation

An area of our process is lagging in needed throughput because of inadequate staffing for the current temporary load. The criticality of the situation was emphasized to supervisors, and they were encouraged to use overtime and personnel loans to resolve the problem. A few days later, I became aware that the plan was followed for a couple of days and then partially abandoned. I readdressed the situation with the specific supervisor, but was frustrated at not being able to pin down in my conversation how or why this occurred. It was not clear whether some participants in the initial plan didn't understand what made it fall apart; i.e., I don't know that the situation may not repeat itself.

Production manager

To manage the team's boundary you need to work with team members to develop a strategy for the unit, an operating philosophy that links its environment to its mission. As we saw, to do this you need to collaborate with your team to address the following questions: Who are the team's key stakeholders? What are its objectives and strategy? What trade-offs does it face when implementing this strategy? What are the guidelines for helping team members make decisions when facing those trade-offs? What are the team members' roles in implementing and supporting these guidelines?

You can begin this work several ways. You can hold formal meetings and use brainstorming to get people started. Similarly, you can build discussions into the normal troubleshooting conversations you have with your group or with individuals. Because the answers to these questions are likely to change over time, however, you have to revisit them frequently to be sure that your operating philosophy and strategy are aligned with your mission. This means that you cannot wait until formal planning meetings, budget reviews, or performance appraisals to review understandings and agreements. Instead, you should build these questions into your daily interactions with team members. Thus, looking at the vignette just presented, the production manager learns that his subordinates have not taken his request for more production seriously; they have not internalized it as a priority. But the story he tells also suggests that he is unable to find out why. Instead, he simply hopes that it will not happen again.

Similarly, in the previous case of the supervisor who appeared browbeaten, the department manager was unable to talk directly to him and say, "It looks to me as though maybe you feel I am browbeating you into accepting more orders. I don't want to this happen— what are you thinking?" If you stay alive to your role as the boundary manager for the team, you will find that the issues of strategy and guidelines emerge continuously in your transactions and interactions with team members. Work with your feelings and thoughts at these moments to understand the dilemmas your subordinates feel and the role you must take to support their work.

Measuring Performance

I have told the executive staff that when a visitor comes in here, for the first half hour he or she should not be able to tell which of you is from engineering, which is from production, and which is from maintenance. I know that they will take me seriously because I also told them that 60 percent of each person's individual appraisal will depend on how the whole executive staff does.

Plant manager

At the meeting this morning I'm curious about how we did Monday and Tuesday. Are we on track or off track for the week? Jim and Ron say the schedule is now 84 a day. I calculate that if our original number was 69 a day, then we are already behind 51 units for the week. Jim says that the scheduling system only tells what's due today. I'm confused; I want to know how we are doing versus the schedule. I want to know if I should be working faster or helping out in a different place. Are we going to make it for the cutoff?"

Operator on the packing line, part of a team recently given considerable autonomy

Establish Outcome Measures

In working with the team to define its key objectives and priorities, you can help team members understand and track team performance if, in consultation with the team, you can actually develop some informal measures of *team* performance.

Thus, as the first quote suggests, the plant manager is shaping a team system among her executive staff by rewarding each person for team performance. Similarly, as the second example suggests, team members who want to contribute to the management of the team's performance need measures to know how they are doing—not only today, but in relationship to the team's objectives and goals.

Measures of team performance are important because in making the transition to a team environment, you and team members are undoubtedly comfortable with the practices and traditions of measuring individual performance. If you continue to focus on the latter alone, then you may fail to reinforce your commitment to collaboration and coordination among team members. Returning to the theme of the triangle, one way in which you can manage your relationship to the team, as opposed to individual team members, is to measure and reward the team's overall performance as well as the performance of each member. If team members see that you regard these team measures of performance as important, they will begin to take their relationships with one another more seriously.

How can you create measures of team performance? In some settings such measures are easy to come by and may be automatically created as a by-product of the work you do. Thus, a maintenance group may have ready access to the measures of the service it provides, such as downtime of the machines it maintains and average response time to requests. In other settings you may need to spend more time thinking about and developing such measures. An engineering design group may decide that good measures of its performance are the frequency with which manufacturing returns a design for revision (the less the better) or its ability to meet agreed-upon schedules for the delivery of a design.

Clearly, the measures you choose to focus on will be linked to your team's objectives. Thus, to return to the example of the maintenance group, you may decide that in light of your scarce maintenance resources and the growing complexity of the machines that the team has to maintain, you want the machines' users to exercise better care in *using* the machines. Thus, one priority for team members is to teach users about good machine use, and one measure of their capacity to teach might be frequency of requests (fewer) or the nature of the requests (more complex, since breakdowns due to normal misuse decline in number).

To be sure, it is not always easy to construct and create performance measures for the complicated tasks of a team. But experience does suggest three simple guidelines if you should decide to so.

- First, as we have seen, be sure the performance measures are linked to the team's key objectives and priorities.

- Second, don't look for the single best measure; rather, select two or three measures of team performance. While too many measures are as good as none, in selecting more than one, you acknowledge that the team's performance is multifaceted—that it entails achieving several different though ultimately interdependent objectives.

- Third, where possible (and it may not always be possible), use measures that are naturally produced as a by-product of the ongoing work. For example, in the case of a maintenance group, downtime is most likely recorded in plant records, and response time may be easily tracked from phone logs or time sheets. Similarly, you can build measures out of the natural process of work by asking team members who have frequent contact with your team's internal customers to find out how the latter feel about the team's service. For example, if you are managing a purchasing office you can assign team members who interact frequently with internal customers to periodically conduct a simple survey gauging their satisfaction with your team's work.

If you do construct measures of your team's performance you can use these measures to promote team learning. Try the following: After you and your team decide to collect measures of team performance, ask them to predict what will happen. Returning to the example of the pilot-plant technicians, say they create a goal of completing all production runs within four months of a request. If, instead, after gauging their performance, they discover that they are completing runs within an average of six months, they have a good opportunity to learn about how they function and work as a team and how they interact with their internal customers.

To help the team understand the reasons for the discrepancy between their prediction and the actual outcome, you can have them examine the following possible explanations for their error.

The team had wrong information about their customers. The team overestimated the engineers' ability to create sensible run-time estimates. Engineers don't really understand the details of setting up production runs in a pilot plant. They have too abstract a view of the process. The technician team needs to educate the engineers.

The team did not fully understand the structure of its own work. Consequently, it made the wrong decision in treating all production runs in the same way. "Simple" runs entailing a short set-up time can be stopped in the middle, but "complex" runs, which require engineers to change the plant's piping, should not be stopped in the middle.

The team faced implementation problems. The plant technicians did not know how to interview engineers to assure that run estimates were reasonable.

There were unanticipated changes in the team's environment. Facing stiff competition in the specialty chemical market, senior marketing managers want engineers to increase the number of new chemical products they test each year. The scheduling load on the pilot plant has grown dramatically, leading to inevitable delays. The plant has insufficient capacity

As you can see, when they explore the difference between predicted and actual outcome, the team, far from feeling culpable by their lack of success, can learn about how they function, what their stakeholders want, and how they interact with their customers. One value of measures of team performance is that it sets the stage for sophisticated team learning.

Requesting Resources

When Tom West (made famous in Tracy Kidder's description of his exploits in *The Soul of a New Machine*)[2] led his Data General group in building a new mini-computer, he knew he was competing for scarce resources, such as engineering talent and the cooperation of the software group. Data General had invested heavily in its North Carolina division and could not afford to fully support the production of two new computers. West's strategy for securing the resources he needed was to argue that the company and the various support divisions, such as the software group, should hedge their bets. Why invest all their hopes in North Carolina when, with some judicious support of his division (the Eclipse Group), the company had an alternative if North Carolina failed? This strategy helped West secure the resources his overworked and much committed engineers needed.

As we have seen, one of the fundamental challenges and dilemmas you face as a manager is managing from the "middle." You simultaneously look upward to your manager to understand his or her priorities and downward to authorize, protect, and empower

---

2. Tracy Kidder, *The Soul of a New Machine* (New York: Avon Books, 1984).

your team. You face inevitable conflicts in taking this middle role, because sometimes the pressure on you from above may mean that you cannot protect and support your team as fully or completely as you would like.

But whatever the disappointments or difficulties in managing from the middle at any given time, you are obliged over the longer run to try to get your team the resources it needs to do its work. You need to do this not only to support your team, but also to help your manager develop a realistic picture of the level of company resources at his or her disposal. If you don't ask for what you need, but simply accept tasks and schedules requested from above, you are not helping your manager understand the limits and capacities of the system he or she is managing. In the long run, wishful thinking about the level of available resources can only hurt everyone.

You will be in a much better position to ask for the resources you need, however, if you can link your requests to a thoughtful statement about your objectives, your priorities, and the measures of team performance you are using. By linking resource requests to the concrete tasks your team faces, your manager is less likely to view your requests as simply a sign of "empire building" on your part, and more as a realistic assessment of the resources your team needs to do its work.

Indeed, you can use the mission statement and operating philosophy you've developed as the basis for asking your manager for resources you need to *invest* in your team's development. Benjamin Tregoe and Associates describe the experience of how the senior management of Dow Chemical's polyethylene business secured resources for its development. Knowing that many people at Dow believed that polyethylene was a commodity, the managers of the business developed a coherent strategy for positioning it as a specialty chemical. Developing a plan that outlined where they were, where they wanted to go, and how they could get there, they obtained the resources to develop the business in new ways.[3]

Similarly, if you have identified the trade-off between schedules and quality as key to your team's functioning, you can argue that the team would benefit if it could purchase a new software

---

3. Benjamin Tregoe et al., *Vision in Action* (New York: Simon & Schuster, 1989), p. 28.

tool that improves the project-management process and helps reduce scheduling problems. Your understanding of your own trade-offs can help you get resources to facilitate your team's development.

Similarly, you can use your objectives-and-priorities statement and outcome measures to work with your team's internal customers. If you are in charge of a design group and you can clearly show how the trade-off between schedule and quality poses severe constraints on your team, you can then work with your internal customers (for example, a manufacturing group) to help mitigate this trade-off. You and the manufacturing manager may agree that representatives of the two groups need to come together very early in the design process so that the manufacturing organization can assess how producible the design is. If the two groups can agree early in the process as to what is producible, then the design group itself will more likely be able to meet its schedules without compromising quality.

Finally, however successfully you focus on the group's objectives and work, there will be times when you cannot get the resources you need, and your team will face unavoidable pressures. Here is where you must become sophisticated in managing from the middle. On the one side, you cannot simply wash your hands of the matter, as if to say, "Sorry team, I tried hard to get what you needed, but now it's up to you." You have to stay emotionally connected to the stress they will feel. Team members have to know that you are aware of the difficulty of their upcoming work.

But on the other side, you cannot simply align with your team as if to say, "Well, *I'm* with you; those guys up there don't know a thing." As a manager you are implicated in the management process and represent corporate priorities to the team. By aligning with the team against upper managers you may win the short-term approval of team members—you are now "one of them"—but in the longer run, you will lose the legitimacy that comes from being linked into the management process, for being the team's representative to upper management. So to manage *from* the middle you have got to stay *in* the middle, connecting both to your managers and to the team.

Promote an Effective System of Roles

An employee reports a water leak to his supervisor. The supervisor calls the emergency-control room, then checks with the boiler room to see if there has been a follow-up. Boiler-room personnel state that the leak is not their problem and recommend that the supervisor call maintenance. The supervisor leaves a message on the Audix, and 42 minutes after the leak was first noticed, the appropriate response personnel appear to fix the leak. Why did it take so long?

Factory supervisor

An aircraft controller in Miami noticed that a plane was losing altitude. In the status hierarchy of the air-service system, pilots have more prestige than controllers do. Consequently, controllers hesitate to remind pilots of obvious factors or errors. The controller radioed the pilot, "How are things along out there?" The pilot, preoccupied with repairing a circuit and oblivious to his loss of altitude, answered, "Okay, we'd like to turn around and come back in." The plane crashed.

Newspaper Report[4]

Understanding the Role System

As the manager of the team, you manage a role system in which different team members taking up different assignments and tasks must nonetheless coordinate their work with another. Team members together create a system of roles. As the manager, you need to assess whether the system hangs together, whether as each team member meets his or her own obligations, the work of the team as a whole is coherent and each team member's efforts build toward a total team accomplishment.

There are three features of a team's role system that shape how effective the team is in doing its work. The team's role system works when: (1) team members have a clear understanding of their own particular assignments or job duties; (2) they understand the work of other team members; and (3) they feel that they have sufficient elbow room to do their jobs and coordinate with another. Consider what happens when any one of these features of the team's role system is lacking. First, clearly, if team members do not under-

---

4. This case is described in Larry Hirschhorn, *Beyond Mechanization* (Cambridge: MIT Press, 1984), p. 80.

stand their own roles they cannot begin to do their work. But second, if they do not understand one another's roles they cannot coordinate their work with each other, and they will have a harder time regulating their relationships in your absence.

If, for example, technical-support employees on a sales team do not understand the sales process—that is, what customers want and what salespeople have to commit to make a sale—they will be less able to support the salesperson trying to make a sale or manage a customer without a great deal of explanation and direction. They may not know that certain customers, when meeting technical-support people, are less concerned with understanding the full capabilities of a computer system but instead want to the know that the system is reliable in a limited range of uses, and that support services are available to maintain reliability and uptime. If the technical-support person understands this, he or she can then support the salesperson's presentation (or continued management of the customer) more effectively, and the two together *can appear as a team to the customer.* The two need to understand the basic features and challenges of one another's work—not to do each other's work, but to support each other.

Third, and finally, team members need to feel that you are giving them elbow room to work, that you care about their accomplishments, but will let them devise the methods they need to get the work done. This is important not only to help them develop and feel increasingly competent, but because in the absence of elbow room, team members will be unable to solve new problems and challenges that they face together. For example, a production group may find that they face problems because a new supplier is supplying bar-stock that tends to jam some old machines. Whose problem is it, the person in the warehouse who inspects incoming supplies, the maintenance person who might be able to adjust the machines, the operators who could develop a new way of feeding the machine? If team members do not feel they have elbow room to tackle problems that may lie outside their traditional assignments, this new problem is likely to fall between the cracks, and the plant manager will have to take responsibility for solving it. Only if team members feel that they are sufficiently authorized to "bump up" against one another and work out their relationships to solve new problems can the team regulate itself. In the absence of such authorization, team members are likely to look at a new problem skeptically and say, "That's not my job." In other words, team members will take a relatively *narrow* view of their individual roles so that the team as whole is unresponsive to challenges.

The two opening vignettes to this section highlight the familiar dynamics of problems falling between the cracks when people adopt narrow views of their roles. In the first vignette, despite the demands of the situation, production, the boiler room, and maintenance cannot collaborate to solve a potentially serious problem. Similarly, in the second vignette, the controller, anxious not to intrude in the pilot's role space, despite the evident danger facing everyone, does not communicate important information to the pilot.

Commission or Omission?

Team members who act with the knowledge that they have elbow room and are authorized to bump up against each other will be more effective in learning about the problems and challenges the team faces. Consider the following example. Imagine a potential customer calls a sales team to inquire about a new product. The expert on the product is out of the office. If team members adopt narrow definitions of their roles, then no one will want to take the chance of engaging the customer in conversation. Instead, someone might answer perfunctorily, "Please call back when Ms. X returns," as a way of preventing the customer from asking further questions. If the customer does not call back, then there is no trace of the missed opportunity, and the team has lost the chance to learn about the customer's interest.

By contrast, imagine that team members adopt broad definitions of their roles. Then when the call comes in the salesperson will take the call and answer the customer's questions as well as he or she can. Assume for the moment that the salesperson indeed appears confused so that the customer again does not call back. But in this case, the team has much more information about the customer. The trace of the call and the errors associated with it can now be examined so that the team can take better advantage of such calls in the future. In the first case, the error of *omission* produces no learning; in the second, the error of *commission* produces data and a chance to learn.

These cases highlight how a team that feels authorized to bump up against each other will feel so and do so only if they feel that you as the manager value learning and do not punish all errors. People will step into the breech, if and when they are needed, because they are confident that you and the team value action over inaction, even if the chances of success are not immediately high. The team is willing to risk some short-term failures to gain knowledge for longer-term success.

As these examples suggest, you can judge whether you are promoting an effective system of roles by asking yourself three questions:

1. Must I coordinate the work among team members, or can team members regulate their own relationships?

2. Do team members too frequently call on me to troubleshoot new problems, or can they solve new problems themselves?

3. Do team members avoid mistakes and so create errors of omission, or do they take risks because they and the team can tolerate and learn from the unavoidable errors of commission?

If you find that the team members cannot regulate their own relationships in solving old and new problems, and cannot tolerate the errors associated with action, you will find that you have built yourself into a trap. Eager to remain in control of the group, you limit their potential for action. But consequently, they are unable to develop and so leverage your own plans and action. In your eagerness to retain control in the short run, you paradoxically reduce the scope of your control and competence in the longer run. Your team cannot leverage your own efforts.

Three Approaches for Clarifying Roles

How can your team members create and sustain an effective system of roles? In addition to delegating effectively to the team, you need to consider three issues: (1) a specific technique for allocating roles and responsibilities, known as responsibility-charting; (2) ways to ensure that team members take roles without stereotyping one another and thus ultimately creating a rigid role system; and (3) incentives you can use to promote collaboration among team members. Let us consider each one in turn.

Matching Roles and Responsibilities

A small trading firm composed of nine partners has been successful in trading options and futures in the stock and commodity markets. The firm wanted to expand its business into foreign countries, but its informality made it difficult for the partners to develop a structure for managing and tracking this initiative. Typically, everybody was in everybody else's business. But to plan for an overseas expansion the partners had to authorize someone or some combination of partners to plan and then implement the first stages of the effort. They did not need to redesign their formal structure, but rather needed a method for designing a coherent project system for this particular task.

Consultant to the group

Without being notified, and for reasons we could not determine, a (phone) customer had his due date moved twenty days. I called a peer, but feeling that we were pointing a finger at him, he immediately said, "I don't want to hear about it." I then said that I was calling about another customer whose due date had also been changed and was now expecting an answer in an hour. He said that a subordinate of his was at fault. He called her over, and asked her to refer the problem to one of my peers. I then told the customer that we could not yet establish a due date. The customer was naturally upset.

Office supervisor in a phone company

Many work teams confront the problem facing the trading firm described above faced. The team is relatively small, people know their basic jobs, but there are novel situations, stressful circumstances, a repeated sequence of failures, as a problem falls through the cracks, all of which require team members to more carefully clarify their roles and relationships. The tool of responsibility-charting provides a useful framework for examining, elaborating, and ultimately assigning roles.[5]

Responsibility-charting is based on a simple language of accountability. It posits that people can have one of four relationships to a decision: A person is authorized to approve the decision (A); a person is responsible for staffing the decision, for moving it forward,

---

5. Thomas N. Gilmore, *Making a Leadership Change* (San Francisco: Jossey-Bass, 1988), pp. 198–209.

and for providing the data for making it (*R*); a person is consulted before the decision is made (*C*); or a person is informed (*I*) after the decision is made.

In our first example, the trading group assigned an *R* to one partner, who would research the viability of trading overseas; a *C* to two people, who would consult with the first partner; and an *A* to the partnership as a whole, which would decide whether the firm should spend the money to set up the overseas connections it needed to facilitate trading. This simple division of labor helped each partner see what distinctive role he or she had in relationship to the decision and when his or her own participation would be required. In particular, because partners knew that they would individually participate in the final decision to approve, they were able to delegate the *R* role to one of their members. *The responsibility-charting helped them contain their overall anxiety about who would exercise control when and with what power,* so they could more clearly and completely delegate specific responsibility to particular partners.

This method can also help a team clarify when and why it lets problems fall through the cracks. For example, imagine that you as manager are puzzled about why your team cannot seem to launch a successful sales campaign in its region. You can help your team examine this problem using responsibility-charting. Working with your team, you decide that three decisions need to be made to launch the campaign, what campaign theme should be used, which potential customers should be targeted first, and how much money should be spent in the first phase of the campaign.

Examining these decisions, you can ask each team member to say whom they think has what role in relationship to these decisions. Thus you and the team may discover that there is no consensus on who has the *R* for the first decision and that everybody thinks everyone should be consulted on all three decisions. The reason for the stalemate is then apparent. No one feels authorized to staff the team's thinking on the campaign theme, and team members, feeling anxious about the decision structure, want to be included in everything.

Like all techniques, responsibility-charting is most useful when it is internalized by team members, when it helps organize their daily negotiations with each other. As the second vignette shows, the normal flow of work is easily disrupted when people feel blamed for potential problems. The office manager is implicitly blaming her peer in another part of the office, but in the absence of a negotiated sense of responsibilities, people like her peer are likely to feel unfairly blamed when they are asked to explain why an error has occurred. If the team can use the language of responsibility-charting to troubleshoot these typical missteps, team members are less likely to feel defensive when examining a mistake. A language provides a structure, a container for the anxiety people feel when examining a mistake. Thus if the team develops experience with the tool and sees that you are committed to its use, they will begin to use it in spontaneous ways, negotiating *A*s, *R*s, and *C*s with each other as they face ongoing tasks and challenges.

Match Roles without Stereotyping

The rescue squad complained to the chief operating officer (COO) of the hospital that the emergency-room charge nurse did not immediately send a nurse to help them. She seemed "flip in her attitude." The COO, after observing the emergency room for five to ten minutes, concluded that it was not busy and that the charge nurse could have responded to the rescue-team request. I talked with the emergency-room personnel and found it to be busier than he had perceived. I met with the COO. I wanted him to recognize that he may not have "seen it all" and that it is counterproductive to report problems to the nursing staff "days later after a reported problem has occurred" and without conferring directly with them. But I felt he gave no credence to my point of view. He thinks he understands nursing but it takes much experience to interpret the activity of the emergency room. He thinks he has the total picture. I feel very much that the "male-dominance" syndrome is operating in these kinds of situations.

Head emergency-room nurse

Responsibility-charting will help you and the team allocate assignments across roles in a consistent way for any particular project. But how do you evaluate the *pattern* of assignments that the team creates over the longer run? Are the same people always put in the lead roles, and others in support ones? Does one person always wind up doing the technical work for a project, while another manages the key relationships with an internal customer? Is the role system flexible or rigid?

These questions are important because teams will be stronger and more capable of managing themselves if people have the chance to take up new roles as well as perform old ones effectively. A team's productivity grows for three reasons. First, the more people can take up different roles, the more they will understand one another's work, and as we have seen, this alone creates a stronger team. Second, as people take up more roles, they become more capable workers in general and are able to perform old roles more effectively as well as take up new ones. Overall team productivity rises. Third, and finally, as team members become well rounded, the flexibility of the team and its capacity to solve new problems grow.

But while the gains to the team are great when people can take a variety of roles over time, there are powerful forces that tend to pigeonhole people in particular roles and assignments. People are stereotyped. For example, some team members may wish to be stereotyped because they are comfortable staying with the skills they know rather than trying something new. Similarly, facing the pressure of work and deadlines, team members would rather rely on people who are experienced in particular skills or kinds of work, rather than risk giving an assignment to an inexperienced team member. Third, gender, race, age, and ethnic biases may consciously or unconsciously shape patterns of delegation and role assignment in ways that stereotype individual team members. For example, a woman may be put into customer-relations role because women as a group are stereotyped as being good at "care-taking" or "nurturing" tasks, even when the individual woman may have very different interests or talents. Or as the above vignette suggests, a female head nurse may feel that she is not regarded as an authority in her own domain because she is a woman in a male-dominated culture.

These three forces—people's reluctance to try something new, the pressure of the work itself, and group stereotypes—can significantly inhibit the development of a flexible team with members who know one another's work and are growing in competence themselves. But as the team manager, you can limit the impact of these forces by periodically holding individual meetings with team members to assess whether and how they feel stereotyped. In addition, if and when you feel your team is ready, you can facilitate a team discussion in which individual members can discuss their own interests and skills and what new things they would like to learn and the team members could be asked to devise ways to help them.

Project Deadlines

Finally, there are the special problems of giving your team elbow room—of delegating to them—when you and they work within a project environment where *deadlines* shape how people do their work. Much research suggests that halfway into a project, rarely is half the necessary work done. Instead, the curve of accomplishment tends to follow an exponential pattern, rising slowly at first as people scope the problem, work out their division of labor, and confront the hard problems. The curve then rises quickly to completion as the separate but completed parts of the problem or project are finally integrated. Paradoxically, 80 percent of the accomplishments get done in the last 20 percent of the time available to do the work.

Consequently, managers anxious about delegating in the first place will only feel more anxious as they see accomplishment so lagging behind effort. As a result they "hover" over the team and check its work excessively, to the point where team members themselves feel unauthorized to do the work. Team members become less productive, the rate of accomplishment slows down even more, and the now-justified anxiety of the manager rises further. This is an interpersonal trap specific to the dynamics of work and accomplishment in deadline-driven environments. Managers in such settings need to pay special attention to how they respond to the processes of delegation and accomplishment.[6]

Creating Incentives for Collaboration.   One of the most difficult problems that companies seeking to develop effective teams face is creating a reward system that supports team performance. Indeed, companies often find themselves in a contradictory situation, with the senior executives promoting teamwork, yet still depending on a system of individual rewards to motivate and guide behavior.

6. Robert Graham, *Project Management as if People Matterea* (Bala Cynwyd, Pa.: Primevera Press, 1989), p. 29.

To be sure, you as a team manager may have little influence over the corporate reward system, out you can affect the ways in which nonmonetary incentives and rewards shape team members' behavior. Understanding these rewards and incentives, you can then to use them to promote team cooperation.

Consider the familiar findings from research into army platoons. Why do soldiers fight bravely and risk their lives under the most difficult of conditions? Their patriotism is of course an important factor, but most important is their regard for their "buddies," for the other members of their platoon. The research shows that soldiers will sacrifice a lot to simply win the support and good favor of the other soldiers in their platoon. When team members value one another, when they want one another's respect, they will do a lot to satisfy each other. In other words, feeling good about one's place in a team is its own powerful reward.

This means that the more you are able to create a good team climate—a climate that promotes fairness, a sufficient degree of openness, and a context for individual team members to test themselves—the more team members will stretch themselves simply to win the praise and recognition of their team members. *A good team is its own reward.*

Two other nonmonetary rewards also have powerful effects. Just as people want to win the respect of their teammates, they value timely praise from you. It is striking how managers underutilize praise as a reward. This occurs for two reasons. First, managers, particularly managers who have a large portfolio of tasks and want to delegate responsibility to team members, interact with the team around problems and troubles. They are around when something goes wrong, rather than when something goes right. Thus they come to feel that they can manage best, and use their scarce time for management when correcting employees for mistakes rather than praising them for work well done.

Second, in most company settings, the work an employee does is seen and experienced as part of the employee's *obligations,* so that in completing the work, they don't deserve praise. Why praise someone for something they were supposed to do, anyway? But such a perspective overlooks the many creative ways in which employees meet their obligations and the ways in which, in facing new problems, they "rise above the call of duty"; that is, they expand the definition for their official role and take new risks. Naturally, you don't want to go around simply praising people for doing their jobs, but you do want to stay alert to the creativity they use in doing it, to the ways in which they take up new roles and tasks, and to the growth in skills they exhibit as they become more effective.

Finally, such praise is best given when it is given spontaneously, close to the time of performance, or close to the time when you learned about the employee's good performance. Planned praise sounds canned, and the employee, wanting to believe that you mean it, may nonetheless feel that "something is up." Still, although you can't formally plan to praise, you can get yourself ready to praise, you can "stay tuned" to emerging opportunities for praise and when the right moment arrives, give it.

There is one other important form of nonmonetary reward—the discretion or latitude you give individuals or groups to do their work. Most people enjoy controlling the many small but important ways in which they plan and execute their work. Some work best in spurts, others when working steadily. Some like to work from elaborate planning charts and project sheets, others enjoy the freedom they feel when working from memory. Styles of work are as numerous as the people you work with.

As a manager, you must learn to grow comfortable with these different styles, and as you trust the work of individuals more and more you let them work the way they like to, because you know they will get the work done. Trusting them more, you oversee their work less, and over time they feel that they have more choices over how they work and more control over their daily work activities.

This process of *progressive delegation* creates three kinds of rewards for individual team members. First, they have more control over their work; second, they are pleased that you trust them; and third, because other team members see that you trust a team member, that person will win their respect as well as yours. In effect, *delegation is its own reward.*

Finally, in thinking how you can motivate individual team members as well as the team as whole, you may find it useful to ask team members what kind of informal rewards they most value. One, for example, may value the opportunity to go to a company-sponsored seminar, another to have the opportunity to teach a new member some core skills, a third to get more responsibility, and a fourth to be appointed to an interdepartmental task force. If you think your team is ready, try having this discussion with the team as a whole. The more team members know what informal rewards they each value, the more they can begin to informally reward one another. And the more they reward one another, the stronger they will become as a team.

In Sum

Managers know that to create an effective team they have to delegate it sufficient authority. But this is only the beginning. Letting go so that team members can take up more authority will only create confusion, unless you learn to manage the boundary while helping team members regulate their own role relationships. You need to become more sophisticated in managing the relationships with the team's key stakeholders, while team members need to become more sophisticated in managing themselves.

You and your team face four challenges here. First, you and your team need to define an operating philosophy, a strategy for implementing the team's objectives and satisfying its stakeholders. Such a strategy provides guidelines for managing trade-offs, while also highlighting the complementary roles that you and team members take in implementing such guidelines. Second, you and the team need to develop measures of team performance so that the team as a whole can learn from its experience, can assess why, for example, team members did not accomplish what they set out do. Moreover, by measuring its performance, team members can support you as you negotiate for the resources the team needs to do its work. Third, you need to help the team promote an effective system of roles so that they can regulate their relationships without your intervention. Using responsibility-charting and promoting a climate where team members take risks, you can help shape a role system that is both flexible and coherent. Fourth, and finally, working with team members, you can develop a team climate in which the work itself, the relationships that shape how people experience working, and the learning opportunities that work provides can provide powerful incentives for collaboration.

3

Facilitating the Team Process

Key Concepts: Facilitating the group discussion; helping the team generate ideas; understanding how groups get stuck; bringing a discussion to closure; observing individuals in groups.

Facilitating the Group Process

Consultant (Speaking to Will, a Vice President for operations): "Will, I've noticed that you have a very hard time being heard in this group. It's as if you are not allowed to be competent here."

Will (Somewhat huffily): "Yes, that may be so."

Kathy: "Well, a lot if the time I don't talk because Will is saying what's on my mind."

Consultant: "I wonder if you and others aren't using Will in this way. You know, letting him talk for you, saying things you won't say, but then, by not responding, letting him hang out to dry."

> *Conversation at a meeting of the executive strategy group of a company*

As an effective manager in a team environment you need to provide your team with structure, boundaries, a mission, and an effective set of roles. You must also help the team manage its own process, or proceedings. Periodically, your team will need your help as team members face dilemmas in managing the group discussion, generating new ideas, listening to unpopular ones, and making decisions. You face three distinct challenges: helping your team to generate new ideas; helping them to examine these ideas; and helping them to select among them—to make decisions.

Generating Ideas

Groups can employ two useful methods to generate ideas: brainstorming, which relies on a process of unstructured free associations, and the "nominal group technique," which relies on a more rational and structured method for creating alternatives. Let's examine each in turn.

Brainstorming

I was teaching a production team the rudiments of brainstorming. I first asked them to practice brainstorming on a problem that lay entirely outside the world of work: "The lights go out in your house—what might have caused this to happen?" I then asked them to brainstorm on a production problem that was vexing the team, the supervisors, and the plant manager that week. Asked to then reflect on the difference between the two experiences, one worker noted that the second exercise was much harder, "because now we were talking about something we were supposed to know about," and another worker noted her fear of contributing because she didn't want to look stupid.

Trainer

Most managers are familiar with the technique of brainstorming. Using it, groups respond to a question (e.g., Why are sales down? How should work flow be organized?) spontaneously, without regard to the order of speech, the relationships between ideas, and the value of any single idea. There are four guidelines when using brainstorming: (1) The group favors quantity over quality; that is, at this point in the decision process the group wants as many ideas as possible, later it will screen them. (2) Team members should refrain from judging anyone's contribution and should accept any proposed statement or answer—they can ask questions about it after the brainstorming period is over. (3) Team members should avoid censoring their own thinking; they should speak their minds. (4) "Pride of authorship" should be minimized; in other words, team members should feel free to repeat, offer variants, and build upon one another's ideas.

These are simple rules easy to apply, but it is striking how infrequently managers and team members use brainstorming in the normal course of group discussion or group problem solving. Yet when attending a retreat or engaged in some "formal" problem-solving exercise on a task-force team, members can take up the task of brainstorming easily. The difference is caused by how people experience their relationships to one another in the two settings. When facing each other in their normal work roles, they are aware of their status relationships and are sensitive to the ways in which their working relationships affect one another. Thus they are more likely to censor their thoughts and feelings so that they don't make waves. By contrast, when attending a task force or participating in some training course, their normal working relationships are less salient; for example, they may be meeting with people outside their work group, or perhaps all authority has been temporarily vested in an outside trainer or consultant. In this situation they feel freer to say what they are thinking and feeling. The trainer's case described in the vignette tells a similar story. When the group began to focus on a problem that highlighted *their value to the team and the plant,* some members felt more inhibited and some clammed up. This suggests, ironically, that when teams most need to use brainstorming, they are least capable of doing so.

As the team's manager you need to help the team apply brainstorming when they need it the most—at regular team meetings and discussions when you are asking them to work on important problems and issues. This means that first you have to get them to internalize the method and then you have to learn to detect the signs and signals that are telling you that the group needs to free up its thinking. Are only a few people talking? Does the talk and thinking seem stuck? Do you as the manager feel that you rather than the group are doing most of the creative thinking? If you use brainstorming *in response to the immediate situation* you and your team face, rather than as formal tool, it will have more salience and bite, and team members will be more likely to use the technique to develop better ideas, and they will also learn to speak more freely and without fear when working with another on difficult problems.

The Nominal Group Technique. Like brainstorming, the nominal group technique is designed to help a group develop many ideas in response to a problem in a short amount of time. It is, however, more structured, and it is based on the important idea that status differences often interfere in group discussions. The technique thus "nominalizes" the group so that people may speak out without being unduly burdened by status anxieties.[1]

Like brainstorming, the technique is easy to use. Using a key question or problem statement (for example, What are some causes of our production shortfall? What criteria should we use to evaluate our performance? What kind of person do we want for the maintenance job?), you ask each person in the group to write down as many answers as possible to the question. After people have finished writing in silence, you then go around the room, asking each one in turn to state his or her first answer to the question. You write these answers on a flip-chart or blackboard. After each person has contributed one answer to the question you've posed, you go through a second round, asking them to state one more answer to the question. Some people will say that all their answers have already been listed on the flip-chart, in which case you can ask them which answer they would like to underline or especially note, and you can then put a check mark next to this answer. After two or at most three rounds you will have many potential answers to the questions and you can ask the group to survey the list, highlight which answers they would like to discuss in detail, or assess how a particular subset of answers belongs together.

This method is more structured than brainstorming, but it is particularly valuable when you want to give everyone on the team a chance to contribute. Though brainstorming encourages people to express their thoughts freely, without being inhibited by concern about the merits of their contributions, people who are uncertain about their value to the group, or who feel that their status in the group is low still may not contribute. By following the simple rule of going around the room, the nominal group technique eliminates any anxiety that a member may have when facing the choice of *whether*

---

1. Andre L. Pelberg et al., *Group Techniques for Program Planning: A Guide to Nominal Group Technique and Delphi Processes* (Glenview, Ill.: Scott, Foresman, 1975).

and when to talk. When facing difficult problems the process of turn-taking can promote significant anxiety. Should the highest-status member talk first or last? Is the first member who talks being overly aggressive, or is he or she just trying to win brownie points? These primitive feelings, which stem from our earliest experiences in groups, can obstruct participation and free discussion. While less spontaneous than brainstorming, the nominal group technique is designed to help people move past the obstacles these feelings create by providing rules of participation.

Make Facilitating Statements

At a meeting in the CEO's office, Bob, the president, Henry, the vice president for manufacturing, Mary, the marketing VP, George, the controller, and a consultant to this executive team are present. They are having trouble deciding on a test-marketing strategy for their new product.

Henry: "Look, I think our big problem is that everyone here and our direct reports are concerned with their authority. I put myself in that category and also (looking at the CEO) you, Bob."

Mary: "I still don't know what, where, when, and if we've decided to test market the new design."

(Conversation continues about the test-marketing program. The consultant feels that Bob seems visibly uncomfortable, rigid.)

Consultant: "You are all addressing such complex issues here that it is often hard to understand the real meaning behind the words. Bob, Henry said to you that you are overly concerned with your authority."

Bob (leaning forward): "I'm not thin-skinned. I just want to know what he means."

Consultant: "Right. I sense because both of you let this drop, it has been getting in the way of this conversation."

As reported by the consultant to the group

Brainstorming and the nominal group technique help you put ideas on the table. But after using such techniques to get a conversation started, you and the group will return to natural ways of talking and working. In the context of natural conversation, people's relationships to one another, their status anxieties, and their wish to look good, cooperative, or rebellious will all play a role in the shaping the conversation. Sometimes these feelings will facilitate the conversation; sometimes they will obstruct it.

For example, the conversation reported in the vignette highlights a complex interplay between facilitating and obstructing comments. Henry makes a challenging statement suggesting that Bob, the CEO, along with everyone else, is too preoccupied with his own authority to help the executive team really do its work. If true, this statement could help the group find out when and why it is ineffective. But feeling attacked, Bob becomes rigid and looks uncomfortable. Mary, sensing the anxiety, pulls the conversation back to the issue they are struggling with unsuccessfully. The consultant, observing the pattern, decides to make a *process comment* that will help the group clarify how their working relationships may be obstructing their work.

The process comment here has three characteristics. It stops a conversational detour; it draws attention to a problem the group may face in regulating their relationships with one another (the fact that people are too concerned with authority); and it also helps establish a norm that people can talk straight to one another, even if such talk generates feelings that are difficult to manage.

As a manager of a team you may sometimes find it important to make such facilitating statements to help your team reflect on its work, to assess where it is going, or why it is stuck. You want group discussions to be spontaneous in character, and you want people to feel free to think broadly, to challenge one another, and to test their own assumptions. But such a process can also promote confusion and uncertainty. Undirected, a spontaneous discussion can lead team members to lose sight of the purpose of their work. Similarly, the very freedom that people feel to challenge one another can lead some team members to feel, as we saw in the last example, that they are touching hot buttons, getting themselves in trouble, or challenging the implicit political and status system of the team.

How can you help the team balance the gains of spontaneity with the structure that direction and leadership can provide? You certainly don't want to throw out the baby with the bath water—that is, you don't want to impose leadership or direction in a way that kills free discussion. You can use *facilitating* statements that help the team balance spontaneity with structure without creating excessive dependence on your leadership and guidance.

There are two kinds of facilitating statements: those that help the team mark out its progress, giving the team a map of where it has gone thus far, and those that help the team understand why or through what mechanisms it has arrived at a particular point. The former are called "statements of time and scope," the latter are called "process comments." Some examples of each follow.

Imagine that the team is discussing a marketing plan and in doing so realizes that it must assess its experience with its long-term clients. It begins an initially useful discussion of how these clients were acquired, but this discussion provokes some reflections on how responsibility for sales was divided up in days past. The discussion is interesting, but at some point you notice that the old timers are talking more than the newcomers and that, while potentially of interest and useful, this latter discussion has diverted the team, and it is not contributing to the purpose of assessing future marketing plans—it feels a bit too much like "chit-chat." What has happened, and what do you do?

The discussion might have been diverted for several reasons, but consider here the following common process. The task of evaluating the marketing plan may be a difficult one. Some team members, particularly the newer ones, may be anxious about it; perhaps they don't really understand it. The old timers who, quite spontaneously, start talking about the old days are then encouraged to continue their discussion by the anxious ones, who by falling silent simply let them talk on.

No single person or group is then responsible for the diversion. Rather, it is more appropriate to say that the team as whole has cooperated, *without consciously planning to do so,* in taking the discussion off track. Indeed, the unplanned and unconscious nature of the diversion is why the team would find it difficult to get itself back on track, and why they in fact need your help .

Statements of Time and Scope. A facilitating statement of time and scope would simply be one that reminded the team of its primary purpose and so helped it get back on track. You might say something like the following:

> I feel that we are off track here. It was interesting to hear about past arrangements, but we need to stay focused on the key purpose of our discussion—evaluating our marketing

plans. The key issue we were addressing was our relationship to our old clients and how they would respond to this marketing campaign. Let's take the discussion up from there.

Note that this statement has several features.

1. By stating that you believe the team is off track, you are direct. You don't try to get them back *indirectly* by steering the conversation. Instead you state directly and openly that you want them to return to a prior conversation. If you try to steer it and shape it indirectly, you may confuse the team members, and you may also feel that you are fighting the group rather than leading it.

2. You restate the primary purpose of the discussion.

3. You help them get back on track by leading them back to the earlier point in the discussion where they first began to be diverted. You serve as the team's memory of its prior talk.

4. You do not evaluate the contributions to the discussion of any one person or the group. By implication, you make it the entire team's responsibility to get back on track.

5. Similarly, by using the word "we" rather than "you" in describing the course of the conversation, you are collaborating with the group, not judging it.

6. You use the introductory term "I feel" (that we are off track), rather than "you are" (off track) so that you don't foreclose the fact that you might be wrong, or that people don't yet see the diversion. Also in using the term "I feel," you acknowledge that other people may have a different experience than you. By contrast, if you insist that your experience is the correct or only one, your exercise of leadership will create a team composed of passive rather than empowered team members.

Facilitating statements of time and scope can also be made simply to mark out for the group its progress, even if they are not stuck or have not gone off track. For example, such statements as:

"Let me review what I believe we've discussed so far..."

"Let me outline where we have to go next in this discussion..."

"I would like us to spend up to a half hour discussing...and then go onto..."

"I've been tracking our time, and feel that we have spent too much time discussing scheduling. I want to spend just five more minutes on the issue of schedules, and then spend the remainder of our time discussing how we can reduce overtime, irrespective of our scheduling bottlenecks."

Like signposts on the road, these statements let people know where they've come from, and where they are going. You are managing the boundaries of the conversation, and in doing so are helping people to reduce their sense of uncertainty and feelings of anxiety as they discuss difficult and important issues.

This means, of course, that in leading the team you have to be in two psychological spaces at once. You want to contribute directly to the content of the conversation, but at the same time you want to monitor it. And you have to do both. If you talk to the substance of the conversation without monitoring it, you may fail to notice when it gets off track. But if you monitor without talking, you may lose touch with the discussion's meaning and implications, and you may feel unauthorized or unable to shape its direction.

Process Comments. Like statements of time and scope, process comments also highlight how the team may be getting off track or avoiding its work. They do so by providing two levels of explanation: data about the *sequence* of conversation, and provisional *interpretations* or possible reasons of why the team has gotten off track.

Return to our example. Let us assume that you make the statement of time and scope but that the group is still unable to return to the discussion of the marketing campaign. Consider the following process comments you might make:

We seem to have real difficulty zeroing in on our current customers' response to the marketing campaign. We started with it, and we got off track discussing old selling arrangements. I asked us to refocus, and we got off track again. What seems to be the difficulty here?

We seem to have real difficulty zeroing in on our current customers' response to the marketing campaign. We started with it, we got off track discussing old selling arrangements, I asked us to refocus, and we got off track again. *I wonder if there is some basic confusion here about the purpose of the campaign, or why we should be concerned with our old customers, or perhaps there is some other uncertainty?*

We seem to have real difficulty zeroing in on our current customers' response to the marketing campaign. We started with it, we got off track discussing old selling arrangements, I asked us to refocus, and we got off track again. *I had a sense that when we got diverted, the newer members of the team fell silent. Maybe I haven't been clear. Is there something about our marketing practices that I could clarify for you, the newer members; perhaps you don't see how this discussion relates to you?*

These three statements represent a hierarchy of comments. The first simply gives the data about the sequence, leading you to conclude that the team is having difficulty with the conversation. The second offers the interpretation that the group is having difficulty because it is confused or uncertain. The third, pointing to a specific sequence, suggests that the group is having difficulty because the newer members of the team are confused and uncertain. It shows how the group "divided up the work" of diverting the discussion according to different member's relationships to the discussion. It is the most sophisticated of the process comments.

Note finally that all three statements follow the common protocol and spirit of facilitating statements in general. They are nonevaluative, they are collaborative, and they invite further discussion.

Since you have a choice of three levels of process comments to make, which do you choose? As a matter of practice, start with either the first or second levels; they involve the least risk for you, and the least likelihood that some team members in the group will feel judged by the comment. If the team wants to explore the issue of how it got diverted further and you think it is an important learning opportunity for the team, or if after working at the first two levels of interpretation you judge that the team needs to work at the third level to really get on with its work, then go to the third level.

Understanding How Groups Get Stuck

The work of any team can promote much anxiety. People feel uncertain about the quality of their work, the budget of their department, or the impact of changing products on their schedule and requirements. These anxieties, linked to the everyday tasks people have to accomplish, can be compounded when people are uncertain about the nature and quality of their relationships with the people around them. Can they trust the boss or their co-workers, are the political winds shifting, do people mean what they say? These concerns about what people call the "politics" of the company may add to and amplify the normal anxieties and uncertainties associated with work in a fast-changing environment.

As a manager in the team environment your job is to help people contain the impact of these anxieties, to create processes through which people develop a greater understanding of their task environments and feel more authorized and less afraid to take risks in the political environment.

The sources and consequences of anxiety will affect your ability to work with your team, to hold team meetings, and to help your team work together in solving problems. You need to be prepared to recognize when these generalized anxieties are getting in the way of the team's work and learn what you can do about it.

While individuals vary enormously in the way they respond to anxiety, much experience suggests by contrast that groups typically tend to get stuck in three distinct ways when facing feelings of uncertainty, feelings of risk that cannot be expressed, or an implicit or unconscious belief that the group is insufficiently protected or exposed. Teams become "dependency" groups, in which people stop thinking for themselves; they become "fight/flight" groups, in which they attack the manager or leader as a way of escaping from their work; or they create a fight/conformist group in which conformity is valued above everything else in order to defeat an outside enemy. Let's look at each of them.

The Dependency Group

In examining the demise of the *Saturday Evening Post,* Ted Goertzel and Barbara Fiorella highlight the ways in which its founder, Cyrus Curtis, became a mythical figure in the minds of the executives and employees who led the *Post* after his death. This meant that the ways in which Curtis worked, his thoughts, his generative ideas, the physical plant he built, lasted long after his death and long after his polices were suitable to the *Post's* changing circumstances.

"The Curtis Publishing Company became a Philadelphia institution, magnificently housed across from Independence Hall in 'a marble palace built for an eternity of success.' On the family-dominated board no one thought to question the way Cyrus Curtis had done things. Curtis' daughter was wheeled into board meetings at eighty-eight years of age, despite difficulties she had in following the proceedings. One board member was reputed to have maintained an indexed set of board minutes. Whenever a new question came up, it was said that he would consult his notes to find out how it had been dealt with thirty years before. All were comforted by the fantasy that Curtis Publishing Company was somehow immune to the forces that threatened other businesses."[*]

The Psychodynamics of Organizational Failure: The Case of the Old Saturday Evening Post (unpublished)

Imagine that you are leading the team in an analysis of recent sales experiences but you are getting little response from the group. For example, you notice you are doing most of the talking, people take up the tasks you ask them to ("Let's have some suggestions about how to approach this sales campaign") but with little energy, and people who normally have a lot of good ideas are not contributing much. Even people who are usually helpful now seem needy. They want to help, but like inexperienced staffers, they seem to want you to hold their hands. The overall tone is not one of hostility or fighting but rather of passivity and compliance. Looking at your own feelings, you feel as if you seem to be only one who is able to think, that you are *burdened* with the leadership of this group, and that you feel isolated.

The case of Curtis Publishing highlights the dynamics of dependency in the extreme. But as an extreme case it can clarify the more subtle dependency dynamics that may shape your experience as a manager day to day. As the Curtis case suggests, when facing

---

[*] Reprinted with permission from Ted Goertzel and Barbara Fiorella.

difficulty, like a declining market, or a failing product (as was the case for *Post*), people often hope that leaders or authority figures will do their thinking for them, will save them, will do the hard work of transforming the group and reshaping its environment so that the group can develop.

Return to the situation where you feel burdened by the group's unstated dependency on you. What is going on? There is a tendency in these situations to initially blame some single person or another; to imagine, for example, that the person who is typically creative but is now not talking is in fact getting in the way. But typically when the whole group has developed this kind of emotional posture, this valence for passivity and dependency on you, it is a sign that the basic operating or boundary conditions for the group are in some way confused or unsettling for group members.

Confusion typically emerges for three kinds of reasons: anxieties about the context for the discussion; uncertainty about their relationship to potential decisions emerging from the discussion; and anxiety about status relationships in the team itself. Let us examine each one briefly.

First, there may be some difficult questions that underlie the issue or theme you are discussing that people are afraid of or too anxious to discuss directly. For example, in asking people to discuss the marketing campaign, you may have failed to clarify some key questions. Will this affect year-end bonuses? Are we changing our approach to old customers? Will this new campaign be superseded by yet another campaign? These are difficult questions that both you and the group may have avoided addressing simply because they produce discomfort, but left unanswered, these questions color later discussion. Feeling uncertain about their relationships to the underlying events that shape the marketing campaign, group members do not feel empowered to discuss it. Thus, paradoxically, while you may complain that team members do not want to think for themselves, by not working with them to talk about these difficult questions up front, but colluding with them to avoid these questions, you have not helped them to feel empowered—*you have actually helped them become dependent.*

Second, people are uncertain about their relationship to the decisions, if any, that may emerge from the discussion. What are you really asking them for? Are you simply consulting them, but will make the key decisions yourself? Are you trying to build toward a consensus so that the group makes a decision? Do you want them to come up with at least two or three different recommendations? Moreover, some team members may deal with their uncertainty through cynicism, interpreting the lack of clarity as a sign that the key decisions have already been made and that this discussion is pro forma. Team members may, of course, have their preference—they would like to make the decision, or they want to be consulted while you make the decision—but the absence of any explicit contract about their relationship to a potential decision makes it difficult for them to contribute to the conversation.

Third, and finally, team members may be anxious about the status and power relationships in the room. Talking about marketing, for example, may lead them to feel that they are stepping on one team member's turf, or that you are displeased with another team members' performance. These anxieties are most likely to be stimulated if indeed people are uncertain about the context and reasons for the discussion, if they are unsure about your goals in setting up the meeting. Lacking such an understanding, and feeling anxious as a consequence, they typically invent one that invokes the theme of personal conflicts and loyalties on the team itself.

As you can see, the group gets stuck in a very defined way. First, they face some general uncertainty and confusion; second, this makes them anxious; third, this anxiety leads them to clam up, often for different reasons and as a result of different emotional responses. Some become cynical, others afraid, others needy. These different emotional responses are shaped, however, by a common group context, which in turn shapes a common group response—withdrawal and excessive dependence on you.[2]

Do You Know It Is Happening, and What Do You Do?

How do you know are facing a dependency group? We have already described some of the experiences you are likely to face, such as feelings of being burdened and isolated. But you should be aware as you learn to take the management role in a team environment that you may defend yourself against these feelings, you may develop compensatory feelings as a way of not confronting the challenge you face. The most typical compensatory responses to these feelings of isolation are feelings of "victory," "greatness," "the champ," in

---

2. Wilfrid Bion, *Experiences in Groups* (New York: Basic Books, 1959).

which you interpret the fact that you are working alone, without collaborators, as a sign of your special powers to be alone.

Knowing that this is a possibility, you therefore can monitor your own feelings as a clue to what is happening in the group. Do you feel unusually burdened or isolated, or do you feel too much like the "champ of the day"? Consider the latter feeling; it is hard to know for sure, maybe you are just feeling good! But in collaborating with your team *you don't have to know for sure,* you only have to experiment, to check your experience, to test it against the reality that you face and try to act productively in it.

There are several ways to check out what is happening. If you feel that you are talking too much, the smallest experiment you can do is to stop talking. Find the right moment, and say to the group, "I feel that I have been talking too much, so let me be quiet and hear some of your ideas." There may be some ensuing silence and discomfort. If so, *stay with the silence,* don't interrupt it, and somebody other than you will inevitably say something to get the conversation going. If after you have tried this and the conversation begins to feel different, then it is likely that the dependency was shaped by minor rather than major uncertainties, and that the simple fact that the people took the authority to speak after you stepped away leads them to feel more empowered as a group.

But the conversation may not flow so easily, and this may be a sign that larger features of the setting, the context, are confusing people. Here you need to do your second experiment. Say to the group, "I sense that it is hard to talk about these issues. Maybe some of you are feeling uncertain about what we are supposed to be accomplishing here. Let's talk about this. I need to know so that I can use your time productively." Again, there may be some ensuing silence, but stay with it until someone talks and starts the conversation.

As they talk, monitor the conversation for the three reasons why groups may enter into a dependency mode. Don't "give them the answers" immediately—that would only be reinforcing their dependency on your thinking. Use your understanding of the dependency process as well as your own feelings to help you organize your listening, reflecting, and responding to their experiences.

But don't just listen. As you get a feeling for where their major concerns lie, respond as best you can to help clarify the issues that concern and confuse them. "Your instinct is right, I do have to make this decision myself, but I really need your advice and that is why I called this meeting." "Bonus policy will not change, I can commit to that now." And where you, too, cannot guarantee a certain outcome, acknowledge the uncertainty and that it might get in the way, and ask people to work with you despite the uncertainty. "I don't know if this is just another campaign that will go away. I don't believe it is, but I can't guarantee it. But look, let's accept the fact that it is uncertain and work from there."

In Sum

When teams go passive on you they are stuck. While you may first blame one person for this problem, it is likely that the group as whole has developed this emotional posture because the team as a whole is uncertain about some of the key starting conditions for the meeting. Three confusions are typical: confusion about the context, confusion about team members' relationships to the decision process, and anxiety about power relationships in the room.

You can monitor for dependency by assessing your own feelings of isolation or your compensatory feelings that you are powerful because you are working alone. Testing these feelings you can undertake two experiments: first simply talking less or, if that doesn't work, taking the learning role and asking why it seems so difficult to talk. Keeping in mind the reasons people become dependent on you, you can organize your thinking and help clarify their uncertainties and confusions to the best of your ability, acknowledging that even where you don't know the answer, the group can still do productive work.

The Fight/Flight Group

At a partners' meeting the president of a small professional services company announces that because the company has done so well, the next partners' retreat will be held at a "warm, get-away" vacation spot. Hearing this the six partners respond peevishly, with several mumbling that they don't want to go, and that it is unnecessary. The president is taken aback by this response and feels that his leadership has been attacked. He does not pursue the conversation. Reflecting on this conversation a week later, a consultant to the group wonders if the president hadn't stimulated considerable anxiety by his offer. Facing the typical problems of managing their relationships in a small group, of striking a reasonable balance between intimacy and distance, the partners may have been afraid of being too intimate with each other. The president believed they could profit from direct talk in a protected setting, but the partners seemed afraid.

As reported by a consultant to the firm

As the manager of the team you are often the source of difficult work and complicated challenges. You create difficult schedules, shape hard assignments, and expect team members to stretch themselves. Afraid of these tasks, team members, uncertain of their ability to complete them, may quite unconsciously attack your authority as a way of avoiding their work. As the above example suggests, such a group *fights* you because it is in *flight* from its work.

Consider the following situation. A consultant is facilitating the first meeting of a group of middle managers in a R&D group who have been asked to staff a postmortem of a major project. The project was a difficult one. Schedules slipped, people put in much overtime, and upper and middle management communicated poorly. Knowing that a postmortem would stimulate difficult feelings, the vice president for research nonetheless felt that by reviewing its project experience, management could develop better project-management practices.

The first meeting, however, is an unruly one; people appear peeved and irritated, and a manager gets up and attacks both the project and the consultant, arguing that the postmortem will have no consequences and that "this meeting is a waste of time." The consultant turns to the manager and encourages him to talk further and clarify his legitimate concerns. The consultant notes that if the group can't psychologically enroll in the postmortem study, then of course it cannot be meaningful. The fighting manager calms down and later leads a major initiative in the project.

What happened here? The group is anxious about the postmortem; it will stimulate difficult feelings and may not prove profitable. Feeling irritable and at risk, the group then tolerates an attack on the consultant by one of its members, who then becomes its "fight leader," leading the group *away* from its work. The consultant acknowledges the fight leader's concerns and offers him a forum for clarifying his feelings. By doing this the consultant has communicated two things: First, the consultant can tolerate the anxiety that the situation has created; and second, the consultant can collaborate with the manager in the face of the difficult feelings that the task poses.

As this example suggests, *fight* and *flight* go together. Team members are afraid of their work, and feeling powerless and dependent, they create an illusion of group power by fighting you. As the example also suggests, the consultant or manager can confront the fight/flight group by refusing to fight. Instead, he or she acknowledges the anxiety that lies behind the fight stance and provides the time and space for team members to work through and work out their complicated feelings of powerlessness, anxiety, and irritability. Thus in facing this fight/flight group it is better not to interpret the fight as an attack on your authority, but to see it paradoxically as a sign that your team is feeling particularly powerless. By tolerating an attack on you they want assurances that you can tolerate them, as the difficult situation makes them feel anxious or incompetent. By contrast, if you respond testily, if you clam up and fight back, it will signify to them that you cannot contain the difficult, complex thoughts and feelings stimulated by the current situation. This will make them even more anxious, leading the fight-group leader to attack you even more.

The Fight-Conformist Group

Perhaps one of the more paradoxical group processes is one in which a seemingly vigorous and energized group is actually simply conforming. This happens when as a result of a broad range of uncertainties and anxieties of the kind we have already described, the group does not go passive, nor does it attack its leader, but instead it "rallies" behind a single point of view or a particular approach to the exclusion of other points of view or considerations. Like the members of the dependency group, members of this group also stop thinking, but they stop not by going passive, but by signing on too early to a particular stance and then not thinking further. Similarly, like the members of the flight/fight group, they are in flight not simply by "fleeing" the task, but by simplifying it. As the noted writer and management analyst Irving Janis said, such a group is a victim of "group think," in which powerful forces are set in motion to support a particular line of thinking while making it difficult for any people to think of alternatives.[3] Consider the following example, based on a report in the *New York Times* Sunday Magazine.

---

3.   Irving L. Janis, *Groupthink: Psychological Studies of Policy Decisions and Fiascos* (Boston: Houghton Mifflin, 1982).

Under the creative direction of Steve Friedman "USA Today" was touted as a television show that would uniquely tie information and entertainment together to create "infotainment," a form of news appealing to busy Americans. Financed by Gannet, a communications conglomerate, produced by Grant Tinker, recently retired as NBC's chairman, and supported by an ultra-modern production studio costing 40 million dollars, the show was a flop after its first airing.

Interviews with the show's staff highlighted the group dynamics that helped shape this disappointing result. Friedman was a charismatic but temperamental leader. Portraying himself as a rebel and outsider who would transform television news, he helped create a climate of excitement in which subordinates felt they were corporate outlaws ready to destroy the establishment. They were the modernizers, the good guys ready to attack the "bad" producers and directors who did not understand infotainment.

But in supporting Friedman's self-image as an outlaw they also reinforced his arrogance, his disdain for the work and thinking of others. Convinced of his own superiority and brilliance he overlooked some of the most common practices of television production while developing a basic contempt for his audience. Because he disdained bureaucracy he appointed no coordinator to control story development, nor did he hire any professional writers. Moreover, he was convinced that the audience would be satisfied, at least in the first year, with simply glitz. Caught up in this adventure of proving others wrong, his subordinates stopped using their common sense. As one subordinate noted, "we were like a family of alcoholics. Some of us saw what was happening but no one wanted to hear about it."[4]

As the above description of the USA Today Show suggests, Friedman and his subordinates created a fight/conformist group. Supporting his narcissism and arrogance, Friedman's subordinates

---

4. Joe Morgenstern, "Can *USA Today* Be Saved?" *New York Times* Sunday Magazine, January 1, 1989.

lost their ability to think. They came to believe that they had the purchase on the truth and that the rest of the TV world was simply incompetent. As corporate outlaws they would displace the establishment.

Similarly, consider the following. As a lab manager you are leading a meeting about problems of product failure and the talk is slow until someone suggests that the group should really confront the production manager. The idea stimulates you; you know that production processes have been a problem, though you don't know why. The group, sensing your interest, joins the bandwagon and produces a whole host of examples of how the production side of the house has made errors recently. You feel supported by your team and ask for suggestions on how to approach the production manager to help him get his shop into better shape. The group responds with many suggestions, though you notice that certain team members who usually talk have fallen silent. You shrug them off as nervous nellies who don't seem to relish a good fight with the production manager. You are going to stick up for your group even if some of its members are afraid. You feel invigorated. Did you get a consensus? Yes or no?

Much depends on the feel of the process. How did the consensus develop? What role did the group's general uncertainties and dependency on you play in all of this? Who talked and who didn't? To assess whether you have a genuine consensus or not, you need to understand how "group-think" processes emerge, how they are sustained, and why. Five ingredients typically go into making up the "group-think" group and its process.

First, team members face some genuine uncertainties and anxieties, based as we saw on the context of the discussion, their relationship to potential decisions, and anxieties about power relationships in the room. Second, the team, looking for support and certainty, has a tendency to simplify the reality they are trying to assess; they want simple answers in the face of real complexities. Third, this search for simplicity and certainty leads them most often to hope and imagine that in fact your ideas (or some other important team member's ideas) are absolutely correct. Fourth, having then linked an idea to a person, they create a process in which others' ideas are in fact expressions of disloyalty to the person officially or unofficially in charge and so further inhibit creative thinking. Fifth, this whole process is stimulated if the group can identify a "bad" group out there: the other division, the customer who gives you trouble, or a competitor company that is the source of many of the group's problems. In short, in the service of supporting you, reducing their anxiety, and feeling powerful, the team works with you to create a group illusion, a kind of group dream, which represents the group's wishes while distorting the group's reality.

As these components of the group process suggest, you probably got a consensus in the above scenario because a group-think process was stimulated. The team's anxieties first made it feel unempowered, but they could overcome their feelings of weakness and uncertainty by latching onto an idea and linking that idea to you. You then became the victim of the pleasure both you and they take in the feeling of *power that comes simply from unanimity*. The signs that you are valuing unanimity above creative and critical thinking are that certain people fall silent, feeling that were they to talk now they would be attacking you rather than stimulating thinking, and that the group as a whole feels unified in a relationship to some other out-group.

What happens in short is that the consensus is based on a dangerous process through which *thoughts are personalized* and attached to people. The group's illusion or dream is based on a stereotyped cast of characters—the leader whose thought is perfect, the disloyal members who have the temerity to tackle the leader's thought, and the bad out-group or outside person who comes to represent symbolically the source of all the uncertainty and anxieties in the team's environment.

Similarly, consider the following case reported by a consultant.

One of the peculiar aspects of this chemical refinery was the way in which the production team working at the front end was considered the "good-group," while the team working at the back end was considered the "bad-group." The good group had a woman member, called Princess Di, who mothered the group and had picnics for them at her house. The bad group had a "bad" woman who, unmarried and a karate expert, was considered irascible and aggressive. This psychological splitting, which created a good and bad group, made it difficult for the refinery as whole to assess how everyone had contributed to the infrequent but dangerous accidents at the refinery.

This case shows how the features of the fight-conformist group can be combined in complex and counterproductive ways. Refinery workers faced dangerous conditions. To deal with this anxiety they evolved a culture which produced a good group with a good, protecting mother and a bad group with a dangerous "witch." The latter group and woman became the bad "outside," which refinery members could believe were the roots of the refinery's safety problems. The bad group felt very bad about itself, and it willingly took up the scapegoat role; the good group was proud of its elan. Strikingly, what most frightened both groups was the prospect that they would eventually be merged when management finished building a central control room. Neither wanted the "bad" of the refinery to contaminate the "good." As the consultant suggests, the interplay of good and bad prevented the refinery members from understanding themselves as members of a single interrelated system. A complex reality had been replaced by a drama of the good and bad.

The problem with the group-think process is that it is so seductive; it creates the consensus you want and you can easily regard it as a sign of your good leadership skills. This type of team can in fact evolve quite subtly. As a leader you are likely to fall prey to it because it absolves you from managing the group's boundary, for dealing with the underlying uncertainties that bother them, and it converts their potential passive dependency on you to a seemingly vigorous support of you. Yet at bottom both are the same; they both make you and their relationship to you, rather than the work and thinking, the ultimate focus of the group process.

How Can You Detect the Fight-Conformist Group and Guard Against It?

In detecting the fight-conformist group and its emergence, you need to use both your thoughts and feelings and some simple group techniques. The use of feelings is complex here because it would be foolish to regard every team consensus or every excited or energized process as a sign of group think and the presence of a fight-conformist group. Indeed, the team is not necessarily creating a group delusion if it uses feelings of competition with another group as part of the stimulus or the juice for its thinking. Everything depends on the *proportions* of thinking; the key here is balance.

In this context the best indicators are not only an assessment of your feelings—have you been seduced by the power of unanimity?—but also your careful observation of the group process. If you suspect that a fight-conformist group is in the making, then perform the following experiment.

Step out of the process. That is, at a convenient moment step back and say to the team that the idea on the table seems exciting but you want to give more attention to what everyone else has to say. Then keep alert for the following processes.

> Someone steps into your role and assumes to himself or herself the idea that was attached to you. That person substitutes for you so that the team can still have a fight leader, even though you have temporarily resigned from the role.
>
> You notice that as you step out, some people who talk are censored, either implicitly or explicitly—that is, people interrupt them, ignore what they say, or suggest without explanation that they don't seem to understand what the team is really up to.
>
> Feeling authorized by your stepping back, people who have not spoken step in and begin to critique the thinking of the group.
>
> In the latter case, other team members attack those who critique the team's prior thinking or, by contrast, soon after these people have stepped in and spoken, the team unexpectedly appears lifeless and without energy.

If any one of these things happens when you step out, you should entertain the possibility that you are in a fight-conformist group. If two or more of these things happen, then assume that you *are* in a fight-conformist group.

What can you do if you discover you are in such a group? The most important step is to give the team permission to disagree and think critically, and to assure them that you will support them in doing so. But in asking them to change tacks like that, you should not be punitive and attack the prior thinking. After all, you as well contributed to the group-think process, and if you attack them you will only make them feel less powerful, not more. You may also be creating an implicit schism between the now "critical" thinkers and the people who helped create the bandwagon effect in the beginning. Instead, say something like the following.

> I stopped talking so I could listen to the conversation and have the sense that we need to go back a few steps. We are getting

committed to a line of action here, and I just want to check our thinking. Perhaps we were on the right track but maybe we were not.

If after you say this people fall silent, seem deflated, or seem genuinely stuck, then you might use the nominal group technique to reinvigorate the process. Start with the NGT questions: "Consider the assumptions and strategies we have discussed so far. What may be the downside? Where might we be wrong or one-sided?"

The Individual and the Group

Finally, as this discussion suggests, when particular individuals emerge to fight you, join you in a fight, or in some way obstruct the work of the group, it is best not to interpret this as a sign that they alone are interfering with the group's work. People have their own ways of responding to uncertainty and anxiety. Some respond by shutting up, some by fighting, some by trying to make peace when sharply defined differences are important. Indeed, when not facing feelings of anxiety these modes of working in teams are people's sources of strength. Thus, for example, a person with strong empathetic powers can help a group clarify the differences in opinion it faces, but when facing difficulty, he may try to close down an argument prematurely. Similarly, someone who can see many sides to an argument can be powerful when helping the group explore its options, but can be unproductive when she filibusters to stop the group from making a decision.

When a team is working, when you have helped it stay focused on its task, the team as a whole will not support obstructions to its work such as those just described. When the group is stuck, however, when you as the manager have failed to create and sustain the right boundary conditions, then team members will support a spontaneously generated diversion from or obstruction to its work. In such cases the individual is not blocking the group. Rather, the group is taking advantage of the individual's way of responding to anxiety by supporting and reinforcing it. Thus, though you may be tempted to blame one person for the group's problem, it is better to see the person's behavior as a sign that the team as a whole faces a problem and that you as its manager need to respond to it.

How can you do this? Face a person who is obstructing the group's work; limit the person's impact. A direct request is the most effective here. For example, assessing that someone is filibustering because he is afraid of reaching an agreement, you can say: "John, you've stated your position quite clearly, I need to hear what the others think. Hold off your argument for now. If necessary, we can come back to you to assess the arguments we've made."

Or, to an empathizer who is trying to close a discussion prematurely by splitting a decision down the middle, you can say: "Mary, I have the feeling that you are trying to foreclose the argument too quickly. I need to hear more about differences here. Perhaps when we have fully explored differences we can come back to how to put the two sides together."

Note that in both statements, you directly state how you think the people are paradoxically using their strengths and skills to obstruct the team. You ask them to step back in the interests of further work (not because you are upset or angry), and you recognize their skill by suggesting that they can be used more productively by the team later.

Try this. If you find that after you have intervened and gotten one obstructor to step back, the team's work moves smoothly, then it is likely that that person was simply acting out of his or her own personal anxiety. If, however, you find that after you have made your comment, another person steps in to fill the obstructor role, or alternatively, the whole team falls flat because they now see that you don't want to acknowledge their confusion, you need explore with them why they seem confused, why the work seems difficult, why they appear unempowered. This discussion will most likely lead you back to a question of the starting or boundary conditions you have established for the team's work.

Developing Criteria for Assessing Solutions

As you work to the facilitate the team process you will find that in facing some complex decisions the team is ready to assess possible solutions. Imagine, for example, that you and the team are trying to develop a sales strategy to break into a particular marketplace and have discussed the many factors that seem to get in the way of a successful first sale.

At some point, feeling that they understand the obstacles, team members will naturally begin to suggest solutions: invite key managers to a demonstration, get them to meet users of your products in a different though similar industry, or first talk to the people who have to use the product, not those who control the budgets. Disagreements may emerge at this point, and if these are difficult to resolve, the team as a whole perhaps has not yet agreed on the criteria for assessing any alternative. They are disagreeing not only about alternatives but about *the criteria for assessing them.* This is what makes the differences so difficult to resolve.

If and when you sense the team has reached this point in the discussion, you can address this dilemma directly and ask the team to suspend talking about alternatives and come up with a few commonly agreed upon criteria for assessing any alternative.

Thus, to return to our example, some criteria might be, "Any plan must help us get into the marketplace in the next six months," or "A plan is good as long as it gets us a foothold; we don't need a big win at this point." Indeed, in discussing these criteria you and the team members may understand the sources for prior disagreements. Thus, team members who want to convince the direct users first believe that an initial foothold is enough, whereas people who want to go to the top decision makers believe that a big win is necessary to stave off the competition.

To develop such criteria you can use the nominal group technique, asking people to answer the question, "What criteria should we use to assess any alternative?" Or as the manager of the team you can state the criteria you want the team to use. These criteria will then reflect your sense of the requirements of the situation and the team's priorities. In general, any list of criteria should meet two simple standards: There should be no more than two or three criteria; and they should be linked to the team's objectives.

Reaching Agreements

After developing criteria for assessing alternatives and discussing the alternatives themselves, you may find that there are still real differences among team members. To return to the above example, team members may agree that a big sale is necessary, but some will argue that going to direct users will create a "ground-swell" so that the sales process will not be trapped in the normal bureaucratic processes surrounding purchasing activity.

Facing these disagreements, it is useful to think of ways to overcome them. First, you can work on an issue until people arrive at a *consensus*. In developing a consensus, people don't ultimately have to agree on the alternative selected. Instead, those who are in the minority should feel that their views have been heard and considered, that the majority view is sensible if not the best, and that they are now ready to support the majority's alternative whole-heartedly, despite their doubts or preferences.[5]

When reached, a consensus holds the team together and makes it easy for the team to implement the alternative with one voice. But consensus can take a long time to develop. This means that you should try to arrive at a consensus when the decision is an important one, and when you as the manager will depend on the team as whole to implement it. If you must delegate much of the implementation to the team, and if the task is complex, then you should spend the time to develop a consensus. You want all team members to be on board, to own the decision, and to understand it thoroughly.

Conversely, if you are simply seeking team advice for an alternative that you and only a few other team members will implement, or if you will lead the implementation and your team will largely follow your direction, you should not invest the time required to create a consensus, even if you face substantial disagreements of opinion on the team.

What other methods can you use? Three other approaches are useful. First, after listening to the different opinions, you can simply try to strike a compromise among them. For example, in trying to create a sales plan you may decide to invest resources in contacting both the top decision makers and the final users. Second, you can try to stimulate a real debate on the alternatives, asking people, for example, to "make the strongest case you can for your position." The debate itself, the contest between opinions, may bring out unexpected or unrecognized advantages to one position or another. Just as the adversarial system in court forces the two sides to be crisp, precise, and thorough in their arguments, a formal contest or debate, framed as such, can help you and your team make a decision.

Finally, after listening to a wide variety of views you may simply decide to force a solution, using your personal and positional authority to choose one alternative from among those debated. Often, if you don't want to do the work of developing a consensus, it is best to combine the methods of contesting and forcing. You ask

---

5. Jay Galbraith, *Organization Design* (Reading, Mass.: Addison-Wesley, 1977).

people to state their opinions in the most forceful and thorough way they can, and then having heard the best version of the argument for every alternative, you simply decide among them.

In Sum

To help your team do its work, you must learn to facilitate its process. In the old corporate environment, managers taking roles could ignore the team's process, because the team's development, the capacity of its members to take authority, think for themselves, and regulate their relationships with one another, was not important. But today it is. By facilitating the *team's* process, instead of asking it to simply follow *yours,* you create a context and climate for the development of the team and its members.

But as you respect the team's process you also create new complexities for yourself and the team members. *Team processes can go off track.* Thus, for example, in discussing and solving problems team members may be unable to create a climate that promotes their most creative thinking, some team members may suppress discussion in the interests of creating a pseudo-consensus, and all team members may be confused about the nature and sources of their disagreements. The team process can empower you and the team if you help team members confront and overcome the common obstacles to an effective process.

As we have seen, your team is likely to face three basic obstacles as it works to develop an effective process: First, it may lack the tools to promote creative thinking; second, anxieties about the problems they face may lead team members to depend on you excessively, fight you, or turn you into their group-think leader; and last, team members may find it difficult to close out a discussion by using shared criteria for assessing solutions and methods for managing disagreements. To help your team be creative, teach them to use brainstorming and the nominal group technique. To help them manage their anxieties, you should restrain any tendencies you may have to promote dependency, a fighting relationship between yourself and the group, and the group-think process. Finally, to help them close out their discussions, you can help them examine the roots and sources of their differences, and you can promote methods for either reaching consensus or making decisions in the face of disagreements.

Paradoxically, as you step back to give your team more elbow room you step forward into another role where you do the difficult work of helping your team help itself. No longer directing the team, you now facilitate its work. Just as you give up controlling team members, you become more sophisticated in collaborating with them.

4

Managing the Individual

Key Concepts: Promoting a sense of fairness; holding people accountable; providing and receiving feedback.

Promoting a Sense of Fairness

An employee, unsatisfied with the productivity review I gave her, argued that special situations made it difficult for her to complete her work. I said that everyone else faced the same situation, but said I would look into it. She contends that because her levels of attendance and hours are high, my reports are somehow wrong. I can't get her to see that she spends too much time talking and making corrections. But feeling that everyone behaves as she does, she is defensive.

Office manager

This is typical: A department chief makes an exception for a particular employee in violation of standard operating procedure. When asked by a supervisor if this decision applies to others in a similar situation, he says no and gets upset when he is asked to develop guidelines to help the supervisor in the future. He also denies that he makes exceptions. His decisions are unpredictable.

Factory supervisor

The team manager announced that the team would not be getting annual bonuses at the end of the year; markets were slow and sales were down. This predictably depressed the group. Later the manager approached one team member in private and said, "You've been unfairly squeezed out by our overall low performance." He then assured the team member that his especially good performance had been noted and would be reflected in his performance appraisal. When the salary freeze was over, the good appraisal would assure him an above-average raise.

As reported by the manager

One of the central challenges you face as a manager in a team environment is ensuring that team members feel that you are fair. As the chapter-opening vignettes suggest, a sense of unfairness can generate volatile and difficult feelings. This does not mean, however, that you should treat everybody equally; rather, you should acknowledge that people contribute differently to the team, that some members at some times make more valuable contributions and therefore deserve special recognition. In managing in a team environment, you have to acknowledge differences among team members as well as the common tasks and accomplishments that they share. Returning to the concept of the triangle developed in Chapter 1, this means that as you evaluate the distinctive contributions and efforts of team members, you will be developing individual relationships with each team member as well as managing the team as a whole. Thus, as the last vignette in the opening of this section shows, the manager both addressed the problem of team performance and honored the distinctive contributions of one its members.

You can acknowledge differences among team members, you can reward or praise one particular team member who stands out, and still appear to be fair, as long as your praises and rewards do not seem arbitrary. To avoid appearing arbitrary, you should consistently reward individuals for the contributions they make to *team* tasks. If people see that you are ultimately using team accomplishments, rather than your personal likes or dislikes, as the measure of performance and the basis for reward, your behavior will not be considered arbitrary.

In addition, to minimize any perception of unfairness and to help stimulate team productivity, you should acknowledge and reward each team member's developmental accomplishments—that is, you should appreciate the extent to which team members have stretched themselves, acquired new skills, and therefore increased the range of talents and abilities available to the team as whole. Your evaluations of team members should be based primarily on their contributions to the achievement of the team's mission, but you should also reward those who have taken steps to improve their own professional effectiveness. In this way, you measure team members against their distinctive, individual accomplishments as well as against the team's current performance.

Approaching performance evaluations in this way promotes a sense of fairness because people know that in a team members have different talents and skills and that some "start off" more talented or more effective in key areas. People respect those who try hard, who make a dedicated effort to develop their abilities and to stretch themselves to make the team more effective. Most people feel that it is fair for a manager to take into account where individual team members are starting from—to be aware of differences in skills and abilities—and to acknowledge those who work hard to overcome their limitations and thereby contribute to the team. If you reward people based on a combination of two criteria—their *current* contributions to team performance and the degree to which they are stretching themselves so that they can contribute more effectively to *future* team performance—they will see that you are playing fair.

By rewarding and acknowledging people in this way, you are also highlighting your commitment to the team's longer term future. By focusing on how people are developing, and demonstrating your willingness to commit time and attention to this process, you are showing that you are not simply trying to "squeeze out" short-term performance from the team, that you want people to invest in their own growth because that will contribute to the team's longer term flexibility and capability. In doing this, you create not only a climate of fairness but a spirit of commitment as well.

Assessing and Developing Capabilities

How do you help people assess and develop their capabilities? People can develop in different ways, depending on their temperament and wishes. You may not be able to make a budgeting person out of a salesperson, or a salesperson out of an engineer, but specific skills are not the only dimension of development.

Instead, it is useful to think of a person's capability as composed of *four* dimensions. First, what actual skills do they have—are they good at writing, selling, designing, or budgeting? Second, how able are they to work unsupervised and with only general directions set by you or other team leaders? Third, are they able are they to take leadership roles—for example, take responsibility for a project, delegate tasks to other team members and hold the latter accountable for what they promised to do? Fourth, are they able to take up the follower role—that is, can they accept direction from a teammate when the latter has been authorized by either you or the team to lead a team effort?

Different people will face different obstacles in developing along any of these four dimensions. For example, professional employees are often good at working alone and unsupervised, but not very good at delegating tasks, taking leadership roles, or following other peers. Similarly, some people rely excessively on their capacity to delegate and fail to develop certain technical skills that might make them less dependent on other team members. In the extreme, they wind up getting other team members to do their work. Finally, some people have very good technical skills in a certain area—for example, they are good at drafting, or figuring, but they are unable to scope out a significant piece of a project. They can see the details but not the whole picture and are therefore unable to work without close supervision and direction.

Thinking of these dimensions will help you stimulate and monitor the development of team members. Team members do not have to accomplish the impossible—becoming budget people, for example, when their strength is in selling. Instead, you should try to help them improve on at least one of these four aspects of performance. The choice of which aspect and at what rate should of course depend on some combination of the their wishes, your assessment of their capabilities, and the team's longer term needs.

In helping people develop you are challenging them, and because you are often pushing them past their comfort level, some team members may experience you as being aggressive. Some people, after all, are comfortable with their skills and capabilities. If they are good at what they do, why should they try something new? To balance the aggressive stance you may have to take to push people past their comfort level, it is helpful to understand why a person may be uncomfortable in taking up a new role and developing their capabilities.

For some people, situational factors may make development difficult to achieve. When someone is strong and dependable in a particular area, other team members come to rely on that person and may informally reward him or her or for *not* changing. They may even resent it if the team member commits time and attention to developing new capabilities.

Another obstacle to development is that people pride themselves on their competence, and it is often difficult to take up the position of learner, to become someone who must make mistakes in order to grow. Anticipating these mistakes and the likely embarrassment they will feel will cause many people to become anxious when taking up a new challenge.

Finally, people may face personal psychological conflicts in trying to develop along any of the dimensions of capability. For example, some people are afraid of delegating to others; they find it difficult to trust the work of others or have a hard time holding others accountable to a deadline. Similarly, some people may be technically qualified to scope out a project yet feel afraid of working without direction. They are comfortable feeling dependent on someone else, because they don't trust themselves, despite their abilities, or they have an exaggerated view of the consequences of failure. Finally, some people are recalcitrant followers, believing that "bosses" always get in their way. Struggling with authority, they are paradoxically most often comfortable when they are in a "one-down" position, and they have difficulty taking a leadership role.

When coaching or appraising a team member it is useful to keep these possible reasons for resistance in mind, but you are not expected to be a psychologist, and you should think of these possible reasons for reluctance to develop as a simple mental checklist. These points can help you focus the conversation and establish a perspective on the issues facing the team member.

Finally, the same anxieties that may limit a person's willingness to develop also shape the pace and scope of their developmental activities. People learn in different ways. Some prefer to take baby steps, moving slowly outward from their present arenas of competence—for example, some people who like direction may need to give it up slowly, each time testing how they have done and how they feel. At the other extreme, some people learn best by jumping into an entirely new arena, without any tentativeness or testing of the waters. The sense of excitement they find being in a new arena helps them overcome the anxiety they feel in trying something new. You can help team members develop by shaping a series of learning steps that fit their individual learning style and make them feel reasonably comfortable.

Promoting Capability

I am trying to get all the receptionists to answer the phone, saying "Logistics Incorporated, this is so-and-so, how may I help you." It's so important for our quality effort and sets a good tone when dealing with our customers. But I am not sure that they all understand this.

The assistant administrator of a central office

Managing in a team environment means that you want to give team members sufficient elbow room to do their work. You can't hover over them as they do their job, but delegating always tests your capacity to trust your subordinates. They won't do their work in exactly the way you would, and as you observe them and compare their efforts to how you might do it, you might feel anxious. Similarly, the process of delegating tests your subordinates' capacity to understand exactly what it is you want so that they can leave you feeling confident that they can meet your objectives while working out of your sight.

To give a team member elbow room while trusting that person to do the work correctly, it useful for the two of you to clarify the *outcomes* or *accomplishments* you expect as part of team membership. This sounds simple, but frequently managers confuse an outcome with an *activity* or *procedure*. For example, I may tell a secretary that the job is to answer the phone, but in so doing I am describing a procedure, an activity, rather than what outcome I expect from the "phone-answering" activity. By contrast, if I tell the secretary to "help create a climate of responsiveness and helpfulness" when answering the phone, then I am specifying the goal or outcome of the activities. Thus, as the assistant administrator notes in the vignette opening this section, receptionists' accomplishments are linked to the way in which they answer the phone, the tone they set, and their ability to sound helpful. They are not simply being asked to answer the phone and take messages; these duties are intermediate activities, which help create a desired accomplishment or outcome.

Moreover, in specifying an outcome I am also providing the receptionist with a broader arena for exercising discretion and responsibility. There are several ways in which a receptionist might provide a climate of "responsiveness and helpfulness"; examples include making sure that the whereabouts of the key people on a particular day are known and or having on hand a list of phone numbers to use when a caller must be transferred to another office. By contrast, the activity "answer the phone" provides little scope for the imagination; all it means is pick up the horn and say the name of the department or office.

You can discover this distinction between procedure and outcome in many arenas of work. For example, in effective sales organizations, salespeople are typically held accountable for making a dollar number of sales per month or per year, not for making a number of sales calls. The former is the outcome, the latter the activity or procedure.

There are two other guidelines to specifying outcomes that you should keep in mind when helping team members understand their role and when delegating tasks to them. First, a team member must have control over the outcome you have specified. To return to the case of the secretary, if the outcome were specified as "create happy customers," then it clearly would be unrealistic. The secretary controls only a small part of the process that shapes whether or not a customer is happy. The secretary contributes to that process, but certainly does not control it.

To cite another example: Customers calling the office to complain will naturally be unhappy to begin with, and will be placated only if the problems underlying their complaints are in some way resolved. The receptionist does control some *features* of the process of making customers happy—for example, frequently being the first person the customer contacts, a receptionist can help shape important first impressions of the department's capacity to provide good service. Since people calling the office frequently need help in getting linked up with the right person, the receptionist will create a good first impression by knowing the names and numbers of all personnel, where they are, and when they are expected to return. In accomplishing these objectives, the receptionist creates a first impression of helpfulness and responsiveness.

Similarly, consider the case of a salesperson for a soap company whose primary task is to maintain accounts at several supermarkets. Salespeople have little control over the volume of sales to a supermarket—that depends on the price and the features of competing brands—but they can affect how the brand is displayed in the supermarket. Thus we might measure a salesperson's performance based on the number of times he or she can convince the supermarket manager to display the soap in a good location because good display locations have a direct correlation with increased sales.

The second guideline to keep in mind in specifying outcomes for team members is to link a person's goals to the team's overall goals and objectives. If I want to specify the receptionist's expected outcomes, I first need to think about the larger team goal to which that person will contribute. If I want happy customers, then I must think how the receptionist contributes to this outcome through his or her activity.

By contrast, if I am running an office or department whose function is to screen or protect an executive group from undue requests, I will specify the secretary's expected accomplishments very differently; for example, "convey a sense of scarcity of time and attention," or "help create a climate of discipline with courtesy." These specific outcomes will lead the receptionist to develop a set of practices very different from those in the first case. By helping any team member see the link between his or her efforts and the wider department function you enable that person to think and act more imaginatively in assuming their role.

Generally, in thinking about team members' links to the overall team task it is useful to think in terms of relationships. First, some team members directly contribute to a specific "chain" along the "value-added" trail. For example, in designing and manufacturing a new part, a designer works at the front end and a manufacturing supervisor at the back end of the value-adding chain. Second, some team members function in a support role to others, whose work contributes directly to the chain of value-adding activities. For example, a secretary in a sales department does not directly make any sales, but does support the sales process. Similarly, a maintenance technician does not sketch designs, but contributes to the design process by ensuring that computer systems are down only a small fraction of the time. Third, some team members contribute to the longer term as opposed to the short-term accomplishments of the team. As a manager, you may, for example, assign an engineer the task of assessing how new technologies may affect your department's work in the future. The engineer's accomplishment would be to help the department be prepared if necessary to adapt to new technologies as they develop. You would not assess the engineer's performance on the basis of a contribution to current design work.

Appraising Performance

The three key dimensions of defining accountability—specifying an outcome, assessing how the team member can affect it, and linking it to overall team performance—can guide your thinking when you coach and appraise team members. If a team member seems to be having problems in performing effectively, you can find out how you as the manager may be contributing to the difficulty by asking:

Have I specified a clear outcome for the team member?

Can the team member actually control the outcome I have specified?

Does the team member understand where his or her contribution fits into the overall team task?

Moreover, the work you do to develop expected outcomes for team members can be used periodically to appraise their effort, to give them timely feedback on their performance.

Of course, in giving timely feedback you should follow the customary rules and practices for doing this. The first rule is to give feedback frequently, and don't wait until a formal appraisal session to discuss performance. Give the feedback close to the time of a task performance that you actually observed so that the event is fresh in your mind and the team member's mind. Be specific in your comments, avoiding such generalizations as "you're not thorough," or "you appeared capable." Suggest *why* performance may have been inadequate, if it was. Finally, don't be stingy with praise; use it as frequently as you might use criticism.

Your capacity to shape a team member's performance will be much enhanced if you can link the process of giving feedback to your shared understanding of the team member's expected accomplishments. Your remarks will not appear arbitrary, because they will be linked to the team member's beliefs about how he or she is to contribute to team goals. Indeed, by linking feedback to performance you can overcome some of the familiar inhibitions that managers face in criticizing a subordinate's work.

In some settings and with some roles, managers can define outcomes using numbers. For example, a manager and a maintenance technician may agree that the latter should produce "minimum downtime on the computers," an outcome defined numerically as "no more than 5 percent of the time out of order." Many managers will argue that is too difficult and arbitrary to put numbers around a complex set of performances—for example, the work of a designer or an engineer. This can sometimes be true, but often managers avoid putting numbers on a performance because they are unwilling or unable to specify precisely what they want from a team member; they have not sorted out their own priorities, or they are facing conflicting priorities and uncertainties and would rather leave it to the employee to figure out.

If you want to put a number on a team member's performance, one way to get around the problem of performance complexity is to think of two or three different measures of his or her performance, each reflecting a different aspect or dimension of the work. Thus, for example, in establishing the expected outcomes for the work of a designer you might specify the dimension of "rework" and the dimension of "timeliness." The former could be measured by the number of times a design is returned by manufacturing for correction or greater specification; the latter by some estimate of scheduling delays.

You still may conclude that is too difficult or unrealistic to attach numbers to performance, but even the discipline of *thinking* what the measurements might be will help you and your team members develop a much more specific concept of what kind of performance is expected of them. Short of actually measuring performance, it is helpful to ask yourself and your team members the following question: "If we could measure your performance, what would we look at, what would we count, what two to three dimensions of your performance would we pay attention to?" Simply discussing this question with them will help them focus on their core tasks, and over time they may develop their own informal measures of performance.

The Challenge of Negative Feedback

Central Office Administrator: "Ben gave the two new clerks in his office Christmas bonuses."

Vice President for Operations: "What! Christmas bonuses? And these are the people you think we should be firing?!"

Central Office Administrator: "Ben just doesn't want to make waves. He thinks the office is running okay, despite the problems."

> *Observed at a meeting of the executive committee of a mortgage service company*

Partner (talking about a just-completed sales call to a potential client): "I want to talk to you about how you handled the conversation with the client. My sense was that you started fighting with him, as if the way he thought of his problem had to fit your interests. So what do you want?"

Associate (visibly startled and upset): "I know, I know I sometimes feel so inadequate in these encounters that I right away jump to what I know. I just didn't think I was contributing. You had so much more to add."

Partner: "But you are just starting, why would you expect to be competent at this work already?"

(after some silence)

Partner: "I wonder also if I made it hard for you to contribute, perhaps I dominated the conversation too much."

> *As reported by a consultant to an executive-search firm*

The guidelines for giving feedback and linking appraisals to measures of performance are straightforward, yet managers often find it difficult to observe these simple principles, particularly when they have to give a subordinate negative feedback. As the opening vignette to this section suggests, some managers avoid critiquing a subordinate's performance because they don't want to make waves, create conflict, acknowledge differences in the performance of team members, or confront the poorly performing subordinate directly. In other words, they are afraid of the interpersonal processes such difficult conversations create.

Yet, as the second vignette shows, an honest, if somewhat painful, encounter can help each party to the encounter learn much about why and how a subordinate's performance was or was not competent. The partner in the second vignette learns that the associate fought with the client because she felt inadequate, the associate learns that perhaps she expected too much of herself, and the partner speculates that he may or may not be providing the associate with enough opportunities to perform.

If giving negative feedback is really as difficult as most people think, then why was the partner willing to critique the associate's performance? The consultant to the firm, familiar with its key partners and their method of working, suggests that such informal appraisals are accomplished frequently because of the partners' commitment to and belief in the central value of their work. They are passionate about their distinctive approach to executive search. *The internalized authority of the work itself helps them manage the interpersonal dilemmas of the appraisal encounter.* When managers believe in the integrity and salience of the work itself, they can appraise with authority and spontaneity. By linking appraisals to the value and meaning of a performance, both the manager and the subordinate can get in touch with why the performance itself is important. By developing this shared understanding, they are both more willing and able to take the risks of participating in a formal or informal appraisal encounter; they both understand the meaning and value of the work itself.

Getting Feedback

As we have seen throughout this book, you as the manager play a decisive role in shaping your team's performance. *Leadership makes a difference.* That is why languishing departments staffed with employees who are incompetent or who apparently don't care can be transformed when a new manager takes over and provides them with effective leadership and guidance.

Among the most important objectives you should have as a manager is to get feedback on your own performance from your employees. You need to find out whether you are helping them perform. If a team member or a group of team members is not performing effectively, while examining their performance, ask yourself the following questions about your own.

Have I managed the boundary effectively—have I been able to define the team's objectives and my key priorities? Have I been able to obtain the resources the team needs to do its work?

Have I given the team elbow room to do its work? Do the team members understand each other's jobs and assignments? Are the team members comfortable bumping up against each other as they act out their roles in an empowered way? Do they feel authorized to do their work without getting fine-tuned direction from me?

Have I helped each team member understand the outcomes I expect? Do team members individually know where their work fits into the overall team objective?

Have I helped promote a climate of fairness? Have I achieved a balance that enables me to recognize individuals for their distinct contributions, recognize the whole team for its work, and recognize the ways in which particular team members have stretched themselves to contribute (even when those contributions have not yet proven to be measurably significant)?

The best time to ask yourself these questions is when you are meeting with a team member to assess his or her performance. In the course of the conversation you will find occasions to consider together the ways in which your performance as a manager shapes the performance of a team. If you believe the team member has not been sufficiently creative or imaginative, you can ask yourself, "Have I contributed to this problem by not giving the team member enough elbow room or by failing to make clear the connection between individual and team objectives?" Similarly, if a team member is consistently late with work, you can ask yourself, "Have I contributed to this problem by not clarifying where I stand on schedule–quality issues or by not obtaining sufficient resources?"

The table on the next page shows how some of the typical concerns that a manager may have about an employee's performance may be linked to problems in the manager's own performance. To be sure, this doesn't mean that the manager is always at fault or that there are no problem team members. Leadership makes a difference, and it is your responsibility as the manager to find out if and how you may be contributing to an employee's performance problem. When talking with a team member, use this list as a guide

If the team member:	...the manager might consider whether he or she:
Doesn't meet key objectives	hasn't defined priorities, or hasn't provided sufficient resources.
Is not creative	hasn't provided sufficient elbow room, or hasn't linked the team member's role to the team's objectives.
Is not cooperative	has failed to create a climate of fairness.

for getting feedback as well as giving it. In this way you will not only learn about your own performance, you will also help create a spirit of collaboration in the team.

5

Taking the Learner Role

Key Concepts: The paradoxes of management; caught in the "Chinese handcuffs"; seeing yourself as part of the problem; the learner versus the control role; the learner role as an orientation.

The president of the company, who reports to me, has been specially assigned to personally handle the marketing function of the company in the absence of a vice president of marketing. He has been instructed to drop all else and concentrate his energy on sales because our only salesman in one division, who represents half the company's volume, resigned. The president agreed that the proper strategy is to visit each significant customer personally. On Monday and Tuesday, he found various excuses to stay in the office.

The encounter was a telephone conversation late Tuesday in which I asked him if he had visited some customers. He indicated that operations considerations had interfered with his intention to make sales calls. He could tell by my tone and response that I was annoyed with his retreat to the familiar, and I instructed him again to drop everything and go visit customers.

The frustrating aspect is that he knows that this is the most critical need of the company. He agrees he should visit customers, and yet he is ineffective about doing so.

Chairman of the board of a start-up company

91

A group of partners in an architecture firm was meeting at their annual retreat. One partner complained about the behavior of the founding partner. "You always wait until everyone has spoken and this gives you the last word. You can affect our decisions unfairly." The senior partner was surprised. He realized that there were tensions around his participation in group discussions, but that is why he always waited until last. He thought that this way he would not unfairly influence the discussion before the others had a chance to say what was on their mind. In the face of his considerate behavior, he thought that his partners were simply ungrateful!

Consultant to the partners

Throughout we have examined some of the paradoxes of managing in a team environment. The "fight group" that seemingly is attacking you is actually testing you to see if you can be their leader. If you attack the dependency group for their apparent recalcitrance, they will become even more dependent. Your complaints about a subordinate may reflect missteps on your own part. In managing from the middle you protect the group *and* represent your bosses. While managing a team you treat them more as equals, but being their manager means that you take an inherently different role than theirs. While you need to master techniques to help the team do its work, you should incorporate these techniques into the flow of the work so that they feel natural and become embedded in the team's process.

How can you do all this? How can you master these paradoxes and dilemmas? The answer is that you can master them only if you take what we call the "learner role," allowing yourself to experiment, make mistakes, and contain the feeling of being exposed or vulnerable when you appear less than perfect.* By doing this you open yourself to the possibility of seeing and understanding events from the "other-side," from the point of view of people whose experience complements and completes your own. You get to see how you are

---

* For a discussion of learning in organizational life, see Chris Argyris, *Reasoning, Learning and Action: Individual and Organizational* (San Francisco: Jossey-Bass, 1982).

part of the problem, and in this way you become able to resolve some of the traps and paradoxes that stymie you.

Consider the first vignette. The chairman has assumed that he knows what has transpired between himself and the president ("He could tell by my tone and response that I was annoyed with his retreat to the familiar.") But, how does he know this? Imagine for the moment, and this seems plausible, that the president hears only the chairman's profound lack of confidence in him. This reduces his confidence in himself and, while he would like to go out on sales calls, he is simply too afraid to do so. If this is true, the chairman has created his own trap, his own dilemma. As he grows angrier at the president, the president becomes more frightened and is even less able to go out and sell. What can the chairman do?

Think of the Chinese handcuffs children play with. The more we pull to get our fingers out of the hole, the tighter the handcuff becomes around our fingers. The key to getting out of the handcuff is to let go, to stop fighting the handcuff so that it loosens and we can escape. The learner role offers the same outcome. The chairman in the above case is fighting the situation, and by getting angrier he only tightens the situation's grip. He becomes less effective. To take on the learner role he must let go. This means that he must give up trying to *control* the president, trying to make him behave in a certain way, and instead find out why the two of them are stuck in this situation together. Talking directly to the president, he will then discover that he has cowed the president and has thus made both himself and the president ineffective. *In taking a control role you separate yourself from the situation you've helped create. In taking the learner role you acknowledge your participation in it.* Moreover, by taking the learner role and collaborating with those who at first blush are your problems, you increase the chances that they in turn will help you take your role. Your ability to take up the complexities of managing in a team environment is then amplified by those whom you manage. Thus, in the above example, if the president and the chairman can talk directly, the chairman will see how he has cowed the president, and the president, feeling understood, will be better able to respond to the chairman's requests. The chairman will be more effective.

Similarly, consider the story of the architects described in the second vignette. The disgruntled partner complains that the senior and founding partner speaks last in order to control the group. But the founding partner protests that he speaks last to give other partners a chance! Because neither partner has explored his respective contributions to the situation each tightens the situation's grip. The founding partner increasingly resents the disgruntled one for his lack of gratitude, and the disgruntled one increasingly resents the founding partner's attempts to control the group. Each feels increasingly frustrated and helpless because neither can take the learner role to discover how they are contributing to the situation.

Similarly, consider the challenge of managing the dependency group again. Eager to enroll team members in your thinking, you are leading a team meeting but notice increasingly that team members seem uninvolved and uninterested. They answer your questions and are compliant with your requests, but there isn't much energy in their participation. What do you do?

If you take the *control*-oriented approach to your dilemma, you might say to yourself, "This team is not working; people's hearts do not seem to be in it. Something is wrong, and I don't know what is going on, but I need to get control over the situation." Feeling a bit caught, you may add to yourself, "I can't make it look like they (my subordinates) can beat me at this game."

As a result of this inner dialogue, you are likely to take two kinds of actions. First, you may become more commanding in your approach. Instead of taking the "participative" stance, which now seems increasingly unworkable to you, you will behave more authoritatively, almost ordering a particular subordinate to respond to a question or idea you propose. Second, you may feel compelled to fill in for your subordinates' silence, talking more than you normally would, perhaps rushing the agenda along. In both cases your subordinates will continue to behave as before; indeed, you may have inadvertently reinforced their behavior. If you start ordering them, then they will of course wait for their next set of marching orders. If you start talking for them, they will fall increasingly silent. Paradoxically, because you have felt the need to control the situation, you actually reinforce the behaviors that made you feel less in control in the first place.

In both cases you have ruled out the possibility of *learning* about what is actually going on, why your team isn't responding. Feeling that you have lost control, you may assume that you are in a fight with the group and that they can't "beat you at this game." But as we have already seen, the reasons for their silence are potentially numerous. Perhaps you really haven't clarified the task to them, so they don't know what you really want or expect from them. Perhaps they are uncertain about the purposes of the discussion, about its outcome for you and them. Perhaps the group is composed poorly, with certain people feeling that they don't belong at the meeting and others aware of their discomfort but nobody pointing this out.

At one level, taking the learner orientation and *inquiring* seems easy enough. In the above example, instead of becoming more authorative or filling in, you might turn to the group and say, "I feel that I'm talking a mile a minute here, trying to make up for everybody else's silences. What is going on here? Did we stumble somewhere here? Have I confused you?"

But having said it this way, you can see the risks you are taking. What if your subordinates deny that anything is wrong? What if they are embarrassed and unable to say what is on their mind? Perhaps it makes them uncomfortable if their manager acknowledges confusion, because they want their leaders to look "strong." Don't you have egg on your face now?

Moreover, at the moment when you feel that you might lose control, it is not always easy to talk in a calm or even humorous way about the situation. Feeling anxious about staying in control, you might confront the group in a more blaming manner, saying something like, "What's going on? Why do I have to do all the talking here?" "Can't anybody else think in this group besides me?" Or, "I feel like I'm the only one who comes prepared for these meetings. What's wrong with you people?"

Of course, such inquiries are likely to silence a group and reduce your effectiveness even further. But managers often fall into the trap that such statements represent because, feeling anxious about the prospect of losing control, they get angry at those people who are most likely to have the "other half" of the answer, or the missing piece of the jigsaw puzzle.

Yet in taking the risks associated with the learner role, you at least have the chance of improving your performance and effectiveness over the longer run. In asking others to work along with you to understand a group problem, you get more accurate information (for example, you may learn that people didn't talk because they didn't understand the purpose of the meeting), and you can behave with greater effectiveness in the future (by telling them why they are meeting). Moreover, in successfully taking the learner role, you tackle two problems at once. You get better information about a particular dilemma you face, and you also involve your subordinates in a process of collaborative inquiry with you.

In consistently taking the control role, you calm yourself down and feel more in control in the short run, but you never learn why you originally almost lost control. The situation is likely to repeat itself, and will lead to growing alienation between you and your subordinates as a group.

The following table highlights how in taking the learner role you are sacrificing some short-term gains for some longer term results.

	Risks	**Gains**
Learner Role	"Egg on your face" in the short run	Accurate information Improved performance
Control Role	Less ability to improve performance	Feel in control in the short run

The Learner Role as an Orientation

As this table suggests, taking the learner role does entail some short-term risks, but promises some long-term gains. Throughout this book we have described settings and occasions when you can become effective by taking the learning role. For example, in supervising individual team members you can become more effective if you find out how you contribute to their performance. In assessing whether you are a fight-group leader, you experiment by stepping back and observing how the heretofore silent people behave. To promote team effectiveness, you encourage errors of commission. You encourage team members to take the learner role so that they feel authorized to act even when the information they have is necessarily insufficient. In shaping a team strategy, you assess its clarity by seeing if, how, and why team members' confusion is linked to your failure to develop clear guidelines for action. In assessing team performance, you and team members take the learner role by predicting team performance, comparing predicted to actual performance, and then assessing the reasons for any difference between the two.

Think of the learner role as an orientation, a direction. You are heading "north," but there will be times when you reverse directions or take detours. As you work to define an operating mission, facilitate a meeting, get resources for your group, or assess your team's role assignments, pay attention to the moments when you feel stuck, beleaguered, and seemingly trapped by someone who "should" be on your side. Assess whether you can take the learner role at that moment. Can you use your thoughts and feelings in the service of direct talk?

Thus, for example, if you are the president above, can you say something like, "I am irritated, and I don't know what is happening. I ask you to go out and sell and you stay back. Where is the glitch in our communication, what are you feeling? What do you hear me saying?" Similarly, if you are the disgruntled partner in the architecture firm, feeling angry at the founding partner and helpless to change the situation, take the learner role and say to the founding partner, "I'm upset at the way we have discussions here. I feel frustrated. I keep on thinking that you hold back on what you're thinking because you want to have the last word. But I could be completely wrong. What are you feeling?

You may not be able to say these things. You many not wish to make yourself vulnerable in front of others in this way. But *pose the question to yourself; make it an option*. While at certain moments in particular situations you may simply feel too vulnerable, in the end, to develop as a manager, you have no other choice but to master the learner role. To resolve the complexities and paradoxes of managing in a team environment, you must give yourself the chance of learning, being vulnerable, and making mistakes.

Summary

This book has taken you through a series of steps to help you become a more effective manager in a team environment. The following chart reproduced from the Introduction to the book shows the sequence of steps you have taken.

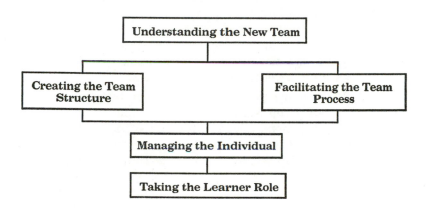

The chart highlights the key knowledge base you need to master and the experiences you need to have to become an effective manager in a team environment.

1. You must understand the dynamics of the new team in which authority is balanced with collaboration. In such a team people do not value conformity and getting along. Instead, recognizing that to take initiative they must bump up against each other, they coordinate their efforts through the practice of direct talk. To do this they use rather than suppress their thoughts and feelings, in this

way learning how each team member can best contribute to the team's work. Team members do not see the team as a family group providing intimacy, but as a work group committed to accomplishing defined objectives.

2. In your role as manager you are responsible for shaping the boundary conditions of the group. This means helping the group understand its strategy and operating philosophy, helping it learn how it is performing, and assuring that is has a flexible system of roles based on ongoing negotiations of roles and responsibilities. In managing the boundary you will be managing from the middle, which means you will face the ongoing struggle of protecting your team while being responsive to your superiors.

3. Even a team with a coherent structure and a flexible role system working to solve new problems as well as manage old ones will face many obstacles. As a manager you need to help the group overcome its dependency and fight tendencies, and provide it with simple tools it can use to generate ideas and make decisions.

4. As a manager you are always in a triangular relationship to your group. While you are the team manager you are also each member's individual boss. You need to promote a climate of fairness so that team members don't feel lost in the group. In exchange for the commitment you make to each individual team member, you must ask each to help develop the team by developing his or her own skills and talents.

5. Managing in a team environment means internalizing and managing the tensions and paradoxes of the management role. If you take the control role, you will be trapped by these paradoxes. Unable to see how you are part of the problem you face, you will fight or manipulate your subordinates or colleagues, decreasing your effectiveness and eroding the trust people have placed in you. You must instead try to take the learner role, making yourself vulnerable to others by acknowledging your own contributions to the situation that you and others face.

If you can accomplish these tasks, you will have helped create a team with the following characteristics.

1. Team members will understand the objectives and operating philosophy of the team.

2. Understanding each other's roles and responsibilities, team members will be able to reconfigure their relationships in response to changing tasks and challenges.

3. Team members will feel that you and team members are fair. Members will not feel that they are sacrificing too much of their own welfare for the comfort, security, or ambitions of others. This sense of fairness will help create a climate of trust.

4. Using direct talk, team members will appreciate one another's strengths and weakness.

5. Team members will appreciate the complexity of your role as the person in the middle. They expect you to support them, but they will also recognize that you must be loyal to your boss as well.

6. Feeling satisfied that the team is organized to do its work, team members will take pleasure in their performance, without expecting the team to meet each member's needs for intimacy.